The New Woman

THE NEW
· WOMAN ·

---

*Feminism in
Greenwich Village,
1910–1920*

---

by
JUNE SOCHEN

Quadrangle Books

A New York Times Co.

To Joyce, Nancy, Patti, Rhoda, and all the women who try to combine the best of old and new womanhood

Contents

Preface

THE EXPERIENCE of those feminists who lived in New York's Greenwich Village during the 1910's suggests at least two larger perspectives: first, it symbolizes the "new woman" who emerged in the early part of this century—a woman who left the home for the factory, a career, and the marketplace; second, it illustrates the dilemma of the cultural reformer in American society. Feminists wanted a wholesale revolution in American values and in the social and economic structure of American life. They rejected modest goals for ambitious ones. But, being Americans, they used a reformer's methods. The difficulties that resulted from the conflict of radical aims and reformer means are recounted in the following pages.

The new woman was a sociological fact by 1910. The Census Report of that year noted that more American women were working than ever before. This also meant that more women were gaining advanced education than ever before. In the academic year 1909–1910, 10 per cent of all Ph.D. degrees from American universities were given to women; by the end of the decade, the figure was 15.1 per cent. Never before had this percentage been matched—nor has it since. To many observers, however, the newfound emancipation of women during the 1910's was viewed with suspicion and even with alarm. Ida Tarbell, for example, the great muckraker, was a traditionalist when it came to freeing her own sex:

> To bear and to rear, to feel the dependence of man and child—the necessity for this—to know that upon them depend the health, the character, the happiness, the future of certain human beings . . . this is their [women's] destiny—this is worthwhile.*

Traditionalists such as Miss Tarbell saw the sanctity of the home threatened. But for every radical feminist scheme, untold numbers of ordinary women doggedly rebuked feminism by living a conventional life. For every suffragist who marched down Fifth Avenue, thousands of dutiful wives tended home fires. For every female trade unionist, armies of young typists saw their work only as a prelude to marriage. For every Jane Addams there were women who perceived good works as meaning membership in the Women's Christian Temperance Union. Much to the dismay of feminists, though more "new" women could be found, women's values remained traditional and acceptable to most Americans—men *and* women.

The decade was no less exciting for the feminists because of this failure. Since their commitment to

* Ida M. Tarbell, *The Business of Being a Woman* (New York: Macmillan, 1912), p. 19.

women's rights was coupled with a conviction that socialism was inevitable in America, they watched the first successful communist revolution with glee. They became pacifists during World War I and often felt that their view of the world was more compatible with that of the new Russian leaders than with that of Wall Street bankers. Although their revolutionary fervor was limited to rhetoric, they frightened potential supporters with their sweeping claims and visions.

Feminism proclaimed the natural equality of women; it challenged traditional roles that Western culture defined as womanly roles. Wifehood and motherhood were too restricting, the feminists argued. A woman's life ought to include more. Feminist philosophers were eclectic: they borrowed their ideas from the eighteenth-century natural-rights school of thought as well as from early twentieth-century anthropology. They had much in common with humanists of all ages who emphasize man's capabilities rather than his dark side or the restrictions of society. The feminist goal was whole cultural reform, not piecemeal, fragmented change. Their problem was to devise a model for radical change that could be used successfully in the United States. That they never found a nonviolent, radical model puts them in the same category with most American reformers who, content with modest legislative change, have fared no better in creating a great society.

The New Woman

❦ 1 ❦

A Stage for Rebellion

GREENWICH VILLAGE in the early years of the century was America's bohemia, the only place a restless, searching, sensitive writer—or writer to be—could find a congenial home. Or so thought hundreds of young men and women who came to the Village from Des Moines, Iowa, or Upper New York State. By 1910 this impression of the Village was well established. Rents were low, and Greenwich Avenue was still "like a barrier flung athwart the Village" which "protected it from the roaring town all about."[1] The Village offered the individual freedom and privacy along with communal activities of intellectual appeal. The Liberal Club scheduled debates on Freudianism, with dancing afterward. Poets were encouraged to read their unpublished verse while dramatists staged impromptu plays. The outside world rarely intruded; gaping tourists did not inundate the Village until the twenties.

During the 1910–1920 decade, life in the Village was rich and exciting. Villagers demonstrated for birth control, encouraged Wobblie leader Big Bill Haywood, campaigned for socialist Morris Hillquit, and spoke out for feminism. Young women joined young men in advocating women's rights and the complete upheaval of American cultural values. Feminism, they believed, involved a complete revision of attitudes and customs regarding women *and* men. It surely meant equal educational and job opportunities, which feminists demanded. Social workers joined writers and teachers in agitating for the elimination of all discriminatory references to women. The feminists of the Village—and most of them *were* feminists in theory if not in practice—found a number of helpful and encouraging Village institutions. The plays of the Provincetown Players, created by Villagers in 1915, depicted the problem of woman in the modern world; and the radical magazine *The Masses* printed editorials and feature articles on the virtues of the woman's movement.

In the 1910's a group of Village feminists worked to achieve a broader and more comprehensive program of women's rights than was advocated by American suffragists generally. While Carrie Chapman Catt concentrated on the passage of state suffrage amendments and Alice Paul, the militant suffragist, worked for the national suffrage amendment, Village feminists asked: And what then? While the suffragist movement narrowed its focus so as to better agitate for the vote, Village feminists debated the broader ideological implications of women's rights. In the nineteenth century, Elizabeth Cady Stanton, the *"enfant terrible* of the suffrage cause,"[2] had thought seriously about the needs of women beyond winning the vote. Nothing short of a restructuring of society, she concluded, would solve the woman's problem. But in the twentieth century the suffragists had no ideological leader to take Mrs. Stanton's place.[3] Village feminists provided the only ideological debate during the early years. The organizational suffragists no longer questioned their long-range goals; they simply agreed with one of their mentors, Susan B. Anthony, that the vote was the key to all of their goals. In practice, this meant that they considered the vote the final step in their struggle for freedom. When it was won, the battle would be over.

Village feminists, however, saw the vote only as a modest stepping-stone to the larger goal: a cultural reorientation that would give all human beings an equal opportunity. Acting counter to the beliefs of most of their contemporaries, they saw feminism as the value system that would accompany the new socialist order. (Later, during the war, they would see feminism tied to pacifism.) Socialism, which accepted feminism as a plank in its official platform, was the Village's pervasive philosophy. Villagers faithfully believed in the eventual transformation of the United States into a cooperative commonwealth. It was only a matter of time. Ida Rauh wagered a young friend of hers in 1912 that within ten years the United

States would be a socialist republic.[4] After seeing the bleak realities of industrialism in the neighboring slums, Villagers were convinced that American workers would not, and could not, tolerate their deplorable working conditions much longer. If good, commonsensical Americans did not legislate immediate reforms—their ardent hope —then laborers would turn to violence. Although Villagers advocated neither anarchism nor violence, they supported the efforts of the IWW and admired the revolutionary journalist John Reed.

The socialist philosophy provided Village feminists with a class analysis for the economic ills of society while feminism gave them the value system they wanted for the culture as a whole. Their view of an egalitarian society— one in which men and women had complete equality of opportunity—was both classless and, in a sense, sexless. Women's roles would be expanded to include many roles traditionally reserved to men. This did not mean the abandonment of women's maternal and domestic roles; rather, women with ability and interest would be allowed to pursue goals beyond the home. Among other things, communal nurseries would be available for professional working mothers. But the special feature of Village feminists was their social view; when they fought for birth control, for example, they did so because family-planning information would give the worker a better chance to determine his fate. Birth-control information was essential to all men and women for the fulfillment of the socialist and feminist ideal.

(6)

Their commitment to socialism made Village feminists open to suspicion by outsiders. Women all over New York City might sympathize with the feminist program of the Villagers, but they were often frightened away by the socialist framework within which it was presented. When Henrietta Rodman delineated the features of her feminist program, for example, she positively alienated most conservative women. For, much to their dismay, Village feminists discovered their greatest resistance not among men but among women. When one of Susan Glaspell's heroines boldly married a socialist to demonstrate her independence, many readers shuddered at the extremity of her action. Mouthing a belief in feminism was the extent of most women's commitment to the cause; but Village feminists never gave up during this decade. They worked tirelessly for the new world they envisioned. World War I rechanneled their energies into peace work, but they saw it as part of their larger conception of feminism. If feminism meant a new culture with more emphasis on human liberty and development, then pacifism was a necessary preface to its accomplishment.

One of the key reasons for the Villagers' interest in the larger aspects of feminism was the community they lived in: it encouraged them to fulfill their individual potentialities. Being part of a community rather than a single organization, Village feminists found support from companions and cooperative groups among their neighbors. They had no need to join an organization that would fulfill their wishes. In minutes a group of Villagers could

[margin annotation: women was not only resistant to men, but other women]

(7)

organize a birth-control demonstration or a march on City Hall. *The Masses* publicized their efforts and the Provincetown Players spoofed them. The many exciting and diverse people in the Village offered the feminists more kinds of activities than a single organization could possibly provide. This was a unique situation. Elsewhere striving women joined the local suffrage association, the Women's Christian Temperance Union, or the women's club. But these groups had limited goals and a narrow interest. They were never arenas for serious discussion of the role of women in the modern world; they offered no comprehensive program based upon a reorganization of the culture's value system.

❦

Among Village feminists, five women were especially typical: Crystal Eastman, Henrietta Rodman, Ida Rauh, Neith Boyce, and Susan Glaspell. Neith Boyce and Susan Glaspell were professional writers whose fiction dealt almost exclusively with the dilemma of the modern woman. Henrietta Rodman and Crystal Eastman were writers and activists. Ida Rauh was a feminist "participator." All of these women viewed themselves as part of a loose group of likeminded thinkers who shared similar goals, and they cherished this camaraderie. They appreciated the good fortune and uniqueness of their situation. They knew that being largely upper middle class in origin, having had the advantage of a college education as well as the freedom to live and support themselves in Greenwich Village, they were a distinctly favored minority. More than this, they were enthusiastic personalities whose zest for life was immediately apparent.

All five women wanted to *do* something. All had read Havelock Ellis, Edward Carpenter, and Sigmund Freud, and knew that the traditional ideas about love and life—especially a woman's life—were being seriously questioned by avant-garde thinkers. They met labor leaders in the Village and heard about the stirrings and unrest of unorganized workers in New York sweatshops. They passed working girls on the street and knew they were leading lives radically different from their mothers'. Knowing all these things, they wished to act upon their knowledge. Their male friends in the Village encouraged them to develop reform ideas and schemes. To the man, the unconventional aims and behavior of the woman were delightful. He liked her because, as Floyd Dell said, she

> was comparatively freed from the home and its influences; because she was more with us, and more like us; because she took the shock and jostle of life's incident more bravely, more candidly and more lightly. She did not put an exaggerated and fictitious emphasis upon things.[5]

The Village feminist group represented several different sides of feminism. All accepted the basic premise that no artificial barrier should impede a woman's development. While all five women were more radical than the suffragists, they differed in degree. Crystal Eastman

career after marriage + children

different views different goals but same cause

love affairs, abortions, out of wedlock

and Henrietta Rodman symbolized the most radical feminist position. They believed that society should be reorganized along socialist lines with cooperative nurseries to care for children. They saw as their goal the total communization of the home. Women would marry, have children, and then enter professional careers to become doctors, lawyers, and engineers.

Neith Boyce and Susan Glaspell represented literary feminism. As professional writers they reflected the popular, romantic view of feminism. They sympathetically portrayed the seemingly infinite yearnings of unfulfilled women. Their fiction resembled much of the popular fiction of the day about the "new woman," but their heroines behaved in more unconventional ways than did standard heroines. They experimented with life in bolder ways— illicit love affairs, abortions, and children born out of wedlock were described in compassionate terms. The literary feminists also drew a human, individual portrait of young women which balanced the hardheaded analyses of Henrietta Rodman and Crystal Eastman.

Ida Rauh was a feminine activist. Accepting the feminist philosophy, she plunged into the hurly-burly world of demonstrations, propaganda campaigns, and arrests. She too had a thoughtful foundation for her activism, but she never wrote out her philosophy. Perhaps the most diversely talented of the group, Miss Rauh lived in both the worlds of the social reformer and the literati. She had read Marx carefully while many of her friends quoted him secondhand. Her feminist friends could count on her to attend a meeting, sign a petition, or lecture to trade-union women. She was comfortable in the editorial meetings of *The Masses*, at an art exhibit of a friend, or at a rally for the Socialist party.

Together these women represented, in the 1910–1920 decade, the most serious effort to work out an answer to the question: After the vote, what then? They did not see the vote as a magic key to woman's freedom. As visionaries and reform practitioners, they wove an elaborate picture of the new world at the same time they tried to chip away at the old one. This concern for both utopian and pragmatic reform made them unique in their time. Their breadth of vision contrasted sharply to the narrow designs of the suffragists. Their optimism and enthusiasm never left them, even when their defeat was apparent.

❧

Crystal Eastman, the dominant woman in the Village group and the most articulate feminist, came from upstate New York. Born in Marlboro, Massachusetts, in 1881, but raised in Elmira, New York, she came to New York City in 1903 to do graduate work in sociology at Columbia University. She was twenty-two years old, energetic, and interested in the world around her. Dark-haired and bright-eyed, her enthusiasm touched everyone she met. Miss Eastman came by her independence, intelligence, and social conscience naturally. Both of her parents were Congregational ministers with strong moral commitments. Her mother, Annis Ford Eastman, typified the new woman. On her graduation from high school in Peoria, Illinois, in 1870, Annis Ford wrote a graduation essay entitled "Oh, Femina, Femina." As her son Max later wrote: "I am sure it expressed the smiling wish that women would buck up and *be something*, and the opinion that it was their own fault and men's loss as well as theirs if they did not."[6] As a mother, Mrs. Eastman conveyed to her daughter Crystal as well as to her three sons the need to stand on one's own feet, to develop oneself as a person, and to make the world a better place in which to live.

Growing up in a rural community was for Crystal pleasant and generally uneventful. She was only a year and a half older than her brother Max, so they were constant companions. The older boys were more distant (Morgan, the oldest, died of scarlet fever at the age of seven). In Max Eastman's memoirs, he continually refers to Crystal's warmth, her sure support of his emotional vacillations, and her devotedness to their parents, all traits that she would exhibit throughout her life. She was a tomboy who frolicked with the boys and planned on leading a life of fulfillment, just like them. After college, it was natural for Crystal to go to New York City—that was where the action was. She wrote to Max: "I am sorry you don't like New York at all. I love it for the people there and the thousands of things they think and do . . . especially the radicals, the reformers, the students—who really live to help, and yet get so much fun out of it."[7] Eventually, Max changed his mind about New York. He came to live with Crystal in 1907 and remained there for a long time.

A *Stage for Rebellion*

Crystal Eastman's first decade in New York was an exceedingly busy one. Living in Greenwich Village and meeting fascinating people, she took a Master's degree in sociology and then went on to law school. She decided on New York University Law School because the dean there was sympathetic to women lawyers; in fact, his sister, Jessie Ashley, became the first woman lawyer in New York. While in law school, Miss Eastman ran a recreation center five nights a week and took her dinners at the Greenwich House Settlement. Her later familiarity with the social worker–settlement house establishment in the city began during her days at NYU. The anarchists, Wobblies, writers, and artists of America also became her friends. Claude McKay, a black poet who was to achieve fame during the Harlem Renaissance of the twenties, called Crystal Eastman "the most beautiful white woman I ever knew."[8]

After law school she took an assignment with the Russell Sage Foundation to investigate work accidents in Pittsburgh. The resulting study, known as the Pittsburgh Survey, established her reputation as a thorough and able social investigator. In 1909 Governor Hughes of New York appointed her to the New York State Employers' Liability Commission, and during the next two years Miss Eastman wrote the state workmen's compensation law. Her talents as researcher and writer, together with her sociological and legal background, proved indispensable for the tasks she undertook. She lived a professionally fulfilling life and believed that other women should have the same opportunities. Her mother had been a suffragist early on; in 1911 Miss Eastman became the campaign manager for woman's suffrage in Wisconsin when the state was preparing to vote on the issue. The experience she gained in this campaign would help her enormously in the next decade, when her energies and talents were directed to feminism and pacifism.

Because she was attractive and vital, Miss Eastman interested men and men interested her. But she was uncertain about marriage. Would she be able to pursue her career if she married? she wondered. It was a question all intelligent, sensitive professional women had to answer. In 1910 she had met a robust insurance agent from Wisconsin named Wallace Benedict, known to his friends as Bennie, who was interested in her and her work. Max Eastman told why he thought his sister was attracted to Bennie:

> His sturdy boyish masculinity, contrasting with something milk-blooded in the cerebral and social-worker types around her, aroused Crystal for the first time physically. And he was one of those rare males—why rare, only nature's perversity can explain—who like to have the woman they love amount to something. His admiring passion gave her poise and confidence.[9]

Meeting of her 1st husband.

But Crystal was not sure. (At the same time, curiously enough, that she agonized over whether she should marry Bennie, her brother Max was debating with himself whether he should marry Ida Rauh.) In February 1911

(14)

she became ill and went home to Elmira to rest and think. Her return to familiar territory pointed up the feeling of closeness she had with her family and her love of the familiar in the face of adversity. From Elmira she wrote to Max:

> I have been feeling very scared about getting married all through this sickness. Getting back to New York and living with you was the hope I fed my drooping spirits on—not Milwaukee and the married state. Your suggestion that if I can't stand it, you'll know it isn't for you, gives me a humorous courage. Perhaps after we've both experimented around a few years, we may end up living together again.[10]

letter to her brother May [handwritten margin note]

Crystal's mother, who had died in 1910, had earlier registered her disapproval of Bennie; she though him too flighty and pleasure-seeking for her serious daughter. But Crystal decided to marry him anyway, and in May 1911, at the age of twenty-nine, she did. They moved to Milwaukee, and in the winter of 1915 moved back to New York. The marriage ended soon thereafter, and Crystal married Walter Fuller, an English impresario, in 1916. With Fuller she had a son and a daughter and enjoyed years of intense social involvement.

married divorce, remarried. [handwritten margin note]

❧

Henrietta Rodman invented "the Greenwich Village whose gay laughter was heard around the world."[11]

She was a charismatic personality who attracted attention to feminism with her sandals and loose-flowing gowns, her habit of smoking in public, and her gatherings at the Liberal Club in the Village. Little is known of her life before 1910. Her parents, Washington and Henrietta Rodman, were native New Yorkers and apparently believed enough in women's education and independence to give their daughter a college education. Henrietta went to the Teachers College of Columbia University and began teaching English in the New York public schools in 1898. For many years she taught at Wadleigh High School until her feminist agitations got her ousted.

By 1910 she was thirty-two years old and a practicing feminist. She retained her maiden name throughout her life though she married a man named Herman deFrem, who remained in the background of Miss Rodman's feminist activities. The couple adopted two teen-aged daughters because, as Henrietta Rodman related, she did not care for babies but enjoyed teen-agers. Her fresh, honest, and often unconventional views delighted and dismayed many readers of the *New York Times* during the 1910's. A picture of her shows a rather large woman with a pleasant-looking face, dark hair, and sparkling eyes that hinted at mischief. Greenwich Village feminism could be fun and serious business at the same time.

❧

Ida Rauh moved to Greenwich Village "to find out about life."[12] The product of a well-to-do Jewish family

in New York City, Ida Rauh left her uptown brownstone
and renounced her wealthy origins to live simply. Max
Eastman described her, the first time he saw her around
1907, as a silent, contemplative, darkly beautiful girl who
"had renounced so hotly all the frills and luxuries of
bourgeois life that she lived almost like a pauper. She
would bring one informal garment, a simple, self-made,
unobtrusively becoming garment and lie in Madeline's
room reading or sleeping all day long."[13] Ida Rauh had
moved in with Madeline Doty, a social worker and friend
of Crystal Eastman's in the Village. Through this mutual
acquaintance Max met her and eventually married her.
According to her own account, Ida Rauh had spent one
day at Barnard College, found it boring, and left. She
heard about a girl who had studied law, so she took the
Regents' examination, passed it, and promptly went to
New York University Law School. It was roughly the
same time that Crystal Eastman was studying there.

Ida Rauh displayed the restlessness and urgency to
action that characterized many incipient feminists of the
era. She was enormously talented but had trouble focus-
ing her energies. Law did not hold her interest; after one
experience in Surrogate Court for the Legal Aid Society,
she decided that practicing law meant fraternizing with
Tammany Hall politicians, something she did not care to
do. She then tried acting, sculpting, painting, and social
crusading; she did well at each enterprise, but then her
interest waned. Her acting with the Provincetown Players
won her critical acclaim, her work for the Women's Trade

does not devote or commit herself

Union League and for the birth-control movement was important and worthwhile; but she never gave herself entirely to anything. Perhaps her restlessness symbolized not only personal unhappiness but the failure of society to prepare women for significant roles.

Ida Rauh married Max Eastman in May 1911, shortly after Crystal married Bennie. After the ceremony Ida Rauh explained to a newspaper reporter what it meant to her. It was something to be through with, she said, to be done so that "then we can say afterward we did not believe in it. It was with us a placating of convention, because if we had gone counter to convention, it would have been too much of a bother for the gain."[14] The Eastmans, each listing their names separately on their mailbox, began married life in the exciting atmosphere of Greenwich Village.

Ida Rauh became a socialist, she later said, after having taken a course on anti-socialism; the arguments were so weak that she decided to become a socialist.[15] She had visited Russia in 1907–1908, had met the great anarchist Kropotkin in Switzerland, and knew William English Walling, the American socialist and reporter. Her associations and experiences convinced her that cooperation, not competition, was the necessary basis for society. During the 1910's she took part in the social causes dedicated to just such a proposition.

❧

The two feminist writers in the Village group were often observers of the Village scene rather than participants. Neith Boyce had come to New York City by way of Indiana and California. Born in Franklin, Indiana, in 1872, she had lived in California for awhile before coming to New York City to write. She took her writing seriously, reporting for the *Commercial Advertiser* during the day and working on short stories at night. Although she was determined to remain free and to devote herself whole-heartedly to her work, she found the newsroom filled with men eager to chase her. One reporter especially liked her. Hutchins Hapgood, a popular chronicler of ghetto life on the Lower East Side and erstwhile writer, fell in love with this quiet, red-haired girl with the green eyes. A dyed-in-the-wool romantic, Hapgood insisted to Neith Boyce that life required rich human relationships and that work, without love, was meaningless.

He convinced her, and in June 1899, at the age of twenty-seven, Neith Boyce married Hutchins Hapgood in Mount Vernon, New York. She insisted that the mar-riage arrangement be tentative: "not to be till death"; rather, "retreat must be easy."[16] Despite this hope, family demands overtook Neith Boyce. Although she would write during the next twenty years, she would also find raising four children, with an impulsive, erratic husband, a difficult, time-consuming job. Trying to reconcile her need to write with the demands of her family was a task that consumed her attention. Later she wrote that she still believed in the concept of a family. "That was something different from individual relationships. You did not choose the family, it happened, and it was more than the sum of its parts. It did not matter whether you liked or

(19)

disliked individual members of it; in trouble the family would rally round."[17]

Two years after their marriage, the Hapgoods had a son whom they named Boyce; Neith was writing a novelette, *A Provident Woman*, and Hutchins described in his memoirs how she devoted a few hours each day to her work. A second son, Charles, was born two years later. With both sons, the Hapgoods went to Europe in 1906 to visit Italy, see Gertrude and Leo Stein, and soak in the culture of the Renaissance. While in Italy, Neith gave birth to a daughter, Miriam. Their second daughter, and fourth child, Beatrix, was born a few years later and completed their family.

After a few years in Italy, the Hapgoods returned to the United States and settled in Indianapolis, where Hutchins helped his brother run a canning business. It did not suit his literary and roaming tastes for long, and in 1909 he took a job with the *New York Evening Post*. The Hapgoods bought a house in Dobbs Ferry and spent their summers on Cape Cod, in Provincetown, where they met the Eastmans, Susan Glaspell, Mary Heaton Vorse, and many others who spent the summer on the Cape. Hutchins commuted into the city every day from Dobbs Ferry while Neith stayed home and cared for the children. Hutchins' Greenwich Village friends sometimes came home with him. Mabel Dodge, the hostess of the famous salon frequented by many Village radicals, recalled in her memoirs how Neith, with her enigmatic smile, appeared to her: "She was like a slow river and her hair was round and round her head in red braids. Her face was white and sweet and she had sleepy, green eyes that sometimes woke up."[18]

Neith Boyce continued to write under her maiden name, a mark of independence which most feminists insisted upon in the 1910's. Her fiction was often published in her brother-in-law Norman Hapgood's magazine, *Harper's Weekly*. Neith's Sphinx-like nature provided an important counterpoint to Hutchins' volatile personality. Mabel Dodge relates an incident which aptly demonstrates the contrast. At dinner one night, Neith and Hutchins were discussing a young woman's love affair with a famous anarchist. Hutchins described the life of this young woman, a serious worker during the day and an illicit lover at night, as her effort "towards the final disintegration of the community." Neith responded "It takes Hutch to see the profound significance of it. To themselves it's merely a job and after the job, relaxation. But Hutchie has to see rebellion and heroism wherever he looks!"[19] In their long and often turbulent marriage, Neith Boyce provided the anchor to Hutchins Hapgood's frenetic wanderings. Her writing dealt with the fundamental problem that all professional and creative women grappled with, and her fiction showed her to be a perceptive recorder of the modern woman's dilemma.

❦

Susan Glaspell began writing as a child. Like Neith Boyce, writing consumed her whole being. Born in 1882 and raised in Des Moines, Iowa, of middle-class parents, Miss Glaspell went to the public schools and then to Drake University. While still in college she sent articles to the Des Moines newspapers; after graduation she became a staff reporter for the *Des Moines News,* which boasted that it was the first Iowa paper to employ women as reporters. In 1900 she had a bylined column called "The News Girl," which related chatty episodes of personal interest to women readers. Miss Glaspell's later writing, her short stories, novels, and plays, would also be about women and directed to them. In 1901 she left the newspaper to devote herself full-time to writing fiction.

Susan Glaspell spent the first decade of the century writing, and for one year she studied at the University of Chicago. She visited New York during the period but always returned to Des Moines. In 1909 she published her first novel, *The Glory of the Conquered.* Two years later she published *The Visioning* and established her reputation as a novelist. In April 1913, at the age of thirty-one, she married George Cram Cook, an Iowa writer whom she had known earlier when he was married to another woman. As she later described it, their love for one another was deep and passionate. Cook shared many traits with Hutchins Hapgood: he too was an incurable romantic who had problems earning a living. As in the case of Neith Boyce, Susan Glaspell's earnings were decisive to the Cooks' economic well-being. They moved to New York after their marriage. "Our friends were living downtown in 'The Village,'" Susan Glaspell later wrote, "so that is where we lived; it was cheaper, and arranged for people like us."[20] With the arrival of the Cooks, and with the return of Crystal Eastman in 1915, the Village feminist group was complete.

❧

These five women had much in common. Three of them were college graduates whose interests ranged from teaching to practicing law. Two were attorneys who had training in social work and law, two were writers with newspaper experience, and one was a teacher. Three came from New York City or somewhere in New York State, while two came from west of the Mississippi. All considered New York City, and especially the Village, as the only place for a vital, searching young woman to live. Most had traveled abroad before 1910 and knew a good deal about European culture. All accepted the right and obligation of the modern woman to love freely and fully; but while they were sometimes romantic about their notions of life, they laced their romanticism with a hardheaded pragmatism. At the beginning of the decade, all five women were around thirty years of age. Neith Boyce had been married for twelve years and had four children. Ida Rauh and Max Eastman married in 1911. Crystal Eastman was deeply involved in drafting labor reform legislation. All of the feminists were experienced women of the world in 1910—sufficiently young and energetic to become engaged in great causes, but old enough to approach their tasks with maturity and knowledge.

(23)

All came from comfortable middle-class backgrounds and had not personally known the bleak realities of industrialism. But living in New York City in the 1910's made them painfully aware of poverty and the grim features of urban living. For the first time in their lives they confronted strikes, intolerance, and destruction. They encountered blind prejudice in their crusade for birth control; in their support of labor unions they were appalled by the intransigence of company management. During the First World War they were overwhelmed by the hysteria and blind patriotism that often chose them as objects for persecution.

The communal experience of the Village feminist group was a unique one in American history. Never before or since has a group of feminists lived in a community so receptive to feminist values, at the same time maintaining ties to the larger American society. The various nineteenth-century utopian experiences were intentionally removed from the mainstream of American life. The Village feminists lived experimentally in the Village but also participated in the social problems of New York City and of the United States. Neither in human contacts nor in human concerns were they divorced from the larger social milieu. Their feminist philosophy, together with their democratic socialist beliefs, contributed thoughtful and relevant ideas to the problem of women in the twentieth century.

The Village feminists did not offer radically original ideas about women's rights, but they did devise new means of implementing their ideas. They also portrayed, in a lucid and forceful manner, the dilemma of woman in an industrial culture. Like the feminist reformers of the nineteenth century, their zeal and persistence never left them. They appreciated the complexities of living in a technical-mechanical culture and they tried, however unsuccessfully, to offer practical as well as theoretical suggestions. Their failure was not due to their lack of sincerity or devotion.

These feminists were a unique breed of reformer. They considered cultural, rather than legislative, reform as crucial to improving society. Although they often used traditional political tools in search of their goals, they ultimately wanted a value revolution in American society. Changing one or two discriminatory laws against women was not enough; they wanted a complete reorientation of attitudes toward women's roles. But toward these radical ends they were forced to use traditional means: propaganda, moral persuasion, citizen education, and direct action. They were inadequate means to solve the mammoth cultural problem they fought. The feminists did not answer, but they certainly asked: How do you create effective cultural reform within the traditional American legislative framework?

2

An Ideology Develops

As ONE POPULAR writer of 1913 carefully noted, most suffragists were not feminists.[1] But some of the younger suffragists did have ideas about broader reforms and greater emancipation. More and more young women were arguing that the vote was not enough; it was only a means to an end, "that end being a complete social revolution."[2] The most articulate and consistent leaders for this feminist position were the Village feminists. They conceived of the woman's movement as a cultural struggle with enormous implications for life in the twentieth century.

Henrietta Rodman and Crystal Eastman were the most systematic thinkers and writers on this subject. Their Village colleagues accepted, as empirically obvious, the truth of feminism and moved on from there. Miss Eastman and Miss Rodman borrowed most of their basic ideas on feminism from Charlotte Perkins Gilman, whom they openly acknowledged as their theoretician. Mrs. Gilman has been called "the major intellectual leader of the struggle for women's rights"[3] during the first two decades of this century. Using an anthropological approach, she argued that American culture was "androcentric," that is, male determined. Man had chained woman to the household since the beginning of recorded history. Without interference or aid from the female sex, he had shaped government, history, economics, law, and religion. Woman had been relegated to bearing children and housekeeping. She had been denied participation in decision-making of any kind because it was assumed that she was biologically incapable.[4]

Mrs. Gilman claimed that women were treated solely as sex objects and not permitted to become human beings. Her goal, then, was to free women to enable them to develop their humanness. Social functions were not the exclusive province of men; working outside the home was not strictly a male function. Women could and wanted to participate in all of life's possibilities. They could not do so if they were regarded only as domestic beings whose biological and social nature confined them to the home. In the twentieth century, Mrs. Gilman argued, women had awakened; they had begun to organize and seek political and economic independence. They did so not to become masculine or to infringe upon man's domain, but to become more human. "They are demanding the vote because they are human," she declared.[5]

Mrs. Gilman believed, as did many of her contemporaries, that the industrial revolution had profound implications for woman and the home. Should not technological know-how be applied to the home? she asked her readers. The principles of industrial efficiency were as relevant in the home as they were in the factory. Specialization and careful differentiation of tasks were crucial to a successful industrial operation; they would be equally effective in the home. The kitchen and laundry areas of each home, Mrs. Gilman observed, produced 90 per cent waste. "Ten skilled experts, working under the proper conditions with proper tools, are not so expensive as a hundred clumsy beginners in a hundred necessarily imperfect average kitchens."[6]

In the twentieth-century home, repetition of plant facilities, as Mrs. Gilman called it, ought to be eliminated; the purchasing power of the home could be used more efficiently by a skilled buyer who would purchase food for several households. In advocating all of these changes in the nature of the household, Mrs. Gilman continually emphasized that they would in no way harm the basic integrity of the home or the "wholesomeness of human life."[7] The changes would produce a more efficient home which would benefit all the family.

While Crystal Eastman and Henrietta Rodman accepted Mrs. Gilman's application of technology to the home, they went one step further. As socialists they believed in the equitable distribution of industrial wealth and in a centralized, rational state in which each individual would be justly rewarded for his work. Industrial planning and maximum productivity would be insured. Similarly, feminism, which held out a hope for the maximum use of human talent, would be properly applied in a socialist state—though not without a fight. In discussing the relationship of socialism to feminism, Crystal Eastman urged every woman to work for the class struggle because "the vast majority of women as well as men are without property, and are of necessity bread and butter slaves under a system of society which allows the very sources of life to be privately owned by a few. . . ."

At the same time, the feminist had to work separately in the sex struggle for her rights. Socialism would most probably provide for feminists, but nothing could be taken for granted. The feminist must count herself "a loyal soldier in the working class army that is marching to overthrow that system," but she must also march in the feminist army to insure her success.[8]

The unfolding of the socialist-feminist state would embrace other interesting features. Because the biological role of motherhood was universal, provisions would be made in the feminist utopia so that working mothers (which, according to Henrietta Rodman, usually meant professional working mothers) would be freed of child-rearing. Experts, qualified and trained in child psychology, would care for children. Not only was this solution practical, but feminists argued that a higher principle was involved: the development of the woman as a complete human being. Since child-rearing called for special knowledge and skill, a mother who was ignorant of the outside

(29)

world was a "child-woman." Henrietta Rodman claimed
that "intelligent mothering" must replace "instinctive
mothering."[9] All mothers, whether full-time or professionals with careers outside the home, required training
which the home did not provide.

If a woman had a well-developed instinct for child
care, she could be a full-time mother once she had special
training. Miss Rodman recognized that "the bringing up
of a child is the greatest creative work of the average man
or woman." And Miss Eastman urged the nationwide
adoption of a motherhood endowment fund so that
mothers who had no economic support would not have to
work but could remain full-time mothers.[10] The job of
child-rearing was considered worthy of the most serious
feminist attention.

The introduction of expert care in child-rearing was,
of course, consonant with Mrs. Gilman's idea of efficient
use of time and talent. Henrietta Rodman envisioned a
culture in which each person did the particular job that
suited him best. Women educated in domestic science
would care for a house; teachers educated in the Montessori method would teach children; articulate and intelligent women would be lawyers or doctors; and each
man would pursue the work of his choice. Since everyone
would be productively engaged, the world's work would
be more efficaciously divided, and everyone would enjoy
more leisure time. What's more, the artificiality of roles
that characterized American culture would be destroyed.
Under an androcentric culture, most roles were reserved

to men while women remained solely wives and mothers. In the new culture of equality between the sexes, these restrictions would disappear. Woman would be trained to perform any task or function that she desired. She would drive a bus, fight a battle, design a building. In an egalitarian socialist society, woman would explore whatever educational or professional field she wished.

Thus, according to feminists, the industrial revolution opened up new cultural opportunities. It offered all women time-saving devices and efficient techniques with which to handle household chores, and it thereby allowed women and men to become whole human beings who might develop their full potential. Under socialism, the inevitable industrial state, an economic transfer of wealth would insure the well-being of every woman and her husband. The worker would benefit as would the woman in the socialist-feminist society. The economic ills of capitalism and the social ills of discrimination would be obliterated. To Crystal Eastman and Henrietta Rodman, woman's opportunities would be infinite once the structure of society and its value system had been changed.

The expansion of woman's roles was tied to another important element in the feminist ideology: the re-education of roles in childhood. The new attitude toward women would begin by retraining all children according to the emancipated values of feminism. Crystal Eastman said that "it must be manly as well as womanly to know how to cook and sew and clean and take care of yourself in the ordinary exigencies of life."[11] No role ought to be regarded as solely a feminine role. It should not be womanly to cry when deeply moved, and manly to repress one's tears. It should not be womanly to change a baby's diaper and manly to refuse to do it.

The male-dominated value system would be replaced with a human value system, which embraced not only child-rearing practices and work opportunities for women but a different sexual attitude as well. The double standard, a male-invented standard, would be ended. "Equal rights, equal responsibilities, equal standards" was Crystal Eastman's slogan for sexual behavior.[12] And Charlotte Perkins Gilman declared:

> Masculine ethics, colored by masculine instincts, always dominated by sex, has at once recognized the value of chastity in the woman, which is right; punished its absence unfairly, which is wrong; and then reversed the whole matter when applied to men, which is ridiculous.[13]

Henrietta Rodman noted that women living in a society of equal opportunity would not imitate men's blunders; they would not smoke or drink or be promiscuous just because of their new freedom.[14] A culture with a single uniform value system would encourage everyone to be honest and responsible.

Feminists hoped to achieve many of their specific aims through legislation. Being evolutionary socialists, they hoped to create the new culture gradually and, if necessary, in piecemeal fashion. Crystal Eastman urged the rewriting of laws regarding marriage, divorce, and inheritance so that the wife and mother would no longer have to depend on her husband. The wife would be a full partner in the business of conducting a household. The law should read:

> You are partners (the Husband and Wife) embarked on the joint enterprise of making a home and raising a family. You have agreed that one shall go out and get the income and the other shall do the work of the home and raise the children. Whatever surplus there is at any time, over and above the cost of maintaining the home, belongs to both of you.[15]

The feminist ideology contained a social and economic analysis of society's defects and a cultural interpretation of man-woman roles in America. This system provided the feminists with a framework within which they could attack a variety of specific evils as well as the whole society. The feminist ideology became, in fact, the basis *and* the justification for many crusades and campaigns. Miss Rodman's feminist apartment house was a direct result of her beliefs; and Miss Eastman's advocacy of birth control was a concrete application of her feminist philosophy. The feminists acted consistently within the socialist-feminist view of the world. The all-inclusive nature of their beliefs enabled them to explain poverty, overpopulation, intolerance, and discrimination. It also gave them solutions to society's problems. Thus, socialism-feminism became a neat package which Village feminists accepted with enthusiasm and distributed for mass consumption.

Although Village feminists enjoyed a measure of success when they addressed themselves to specific social ills, they made no headway in the larger problem of changing America's cultural value system. They could not re-educate boys and girls to the feminist value system with its emphasis upon undifferentiated roles. They could not revolutionize the family structure or the traditional home. They could not force a mass exodus of women into the professions. Their small successes in changing laws did not change the basic habits or values of men and women. While the Villagers thought that the melding of socialism and feminism was appropriate, logical, and exciting, most Americans found this ideology radical and un-American. Terms such as "communal living" implied a revolutionary change that was unacceptable.

❧

In their fiction the Village writers depicted two kinds of feminism: the bohemian, which was usually treated satirically, and the romantic, which was fondly portrayed. Susan Glaspell, Neith Boyce, and Floyd Dell, one of the male feminist leaders in the Village, wrote romantic stories and spoofs about bohemians. The romantic stories were popular and reflected the public's general conception of what feminism meant: a young woman's search for love and happiness. Of course, this was what romantic fiction had always been about, but the feminist stories differed by portraying sympathetically the unconventional behavior of their heroines as being *necessary* and *desirable* in the young woman's search for life's meaning. Village writers agreed with their feminist colleagues that a value revolution was essential. The heroine in their fiction was not educated for a profession and had no special talents, but she wanted something more than motherhood and a home. She wanted an ideology, a program, an experience that would satisfy her, but she was not sure what it was or how to get it. She felt that her life must be different from her mother's, but did not know quite what the differences must be.

As it turned out, the fictional solution was to find the right man and marry him. In this sense, feminist fiction always had a happy ending. The young woman's temporary search for herself was resolved traditionally: she became a wife and eventually a mother. But in her search for fulfillment, the heroine of this romantic fiction practiced her conscious wish for an individual identity—an experience that all feminists knew and one which they wanted all women to have.

Heroines in feminist fiction shared several characteristics: a romantic view of life and love, a burning desire for experience, and a belief in nonconformity. For one of Susan Glaspell's heroines, obeying the rules of life took life from you, and "was that not enough to say against it?"[16] Another heroine ran away with a married man because she believed he was her one true love; a third became pregnant out of wedlock and then had an abortion. Breaking the sexual code of society seemed essential to experiencing life because true love often demanded bold steps of which society was sure to disapprove. As one of Miss Glaspell's heroines said: "Love made life; and in turn love was what life was for."[17] The experience of love was the great experience of life—a truly romantic notion. The quest for love was in fact sometimes all there was to experience: one heroine had sexual relations with a man she did not love because the experience was exciting. "Isn't there anything *else* besides getting married?" she asked.[18] She might be a social worker like her spinster aunt in Chicago, came the answer, so she decided that a love affair was a more appealing alternative.

Sometimes the heroine's search for new experiences produced only disillusionment and greater confusion. Susan Glaspell's heroine Ruth Holland left her lover after living out of wedlock with him for a number of years because she discovered that true love was not permanent. More often the stories ended happily and triumphantly. The woman found real happiness, and the search usually ended with a conventional wedding. As one heroine expressed it:

> All my life I've wanted to *do* something with myself. Something exciting. And this is one thing I *can* do. I can—she hesitated—I can help create a new breed of fierce and athletic girls, new artists, musicians, and singers—.[19]

Susan Glaspell's heroines expressed vague longings. One had a "diffused longing for an enlarged experience."[20]

One of Dell's concluded that life's possibilities were "tiresome, stupid, dull kinds of existence."[21] These obviously impressionable women were the makings of crusaders. Yet Miss Glaspell turned them not into participating females; instead they became, in true romantic fashion, wives whose husbands somehow epitomized true love. Their seemingly conventional lives thus were made to appear novel and unusual.

The heroines of Neith Boyce's fiction were often martyr-like sufferers, women who were victimized by their husbands but who endured humiliation and deprivation. They had settled down to life's expected tasks and accepted, resignedly, their fate. One of Miss Boyce's heroines, who had been abandoned by her husband, was silent when questioned about him. "She could bury her grief and her hurt pride in a proud silence that repelled pity."[22] Another heroine supported her undiscovered genius of a husband by painting miniatures. She never sought pity for the heavy responsibility of earning a living but worked happily to allow her husband the freedom to create. When his talents were discovered, she smiled and noted that the world simply acknowledged what she already knew.[23] These heroines never appeared shrewlike or self-pitying; neither did they seek comfort from others. They had fountains of inner strength, which their irresponsible husbands often tested beyond normal bounds. These women were victims of modern society; romantically portrayed, they were the women to whom feminists appealed.

In all of this romantic feminist writing, the search for love was a purifying experience. Every woman who sought a better life was better for it. The end result was beside the point. To Ruth Holland, one of Susan Glaspell's heroines, seeking love and fulfillment in an illicit love affair made her a "more kind, more generous, more tender" human being. Another character had a hungry quest for knowledge which never brought her economic rewards or personal fame—but it enriched her life and her being.[24] These women, being largely uneducated, could not articulate their dissatisfaction, nor did they have a philosophy to deal with their sterile existence. In true romantic fashion, the hungry, desirous woman knew only one way to satisfy her appetite: with love.

While this dominant theme appealed to Americans' taste for a happy ending, it also fulfilled the feminist writers' belief that woman's search for fulfillment was largely a search for sexual fulfillment. The personal, emotional satisfaction of true love was the object of the feminist quest. The unhappy woman was a woman without a satisfying and permanent lover. Love was the highest expression of human feeling, according to the feminist writers, and its glorious fulfillment created a whole human being. Since feminism sought to provide the woman with deep experience and allow her to become a total human being, true love could easily be viewed as *the* crucial experience, the successful culmination of the feminist search. Satisfaction became equated with love's satisfaction.

An Ideology Develops

In contrast to the socialist-feminist philosophy of Crystal Eastman and Henrietta Rodman, the heroines in Village fiction did not demand equal rights with men— only equal opportunities to experience love. Once they had accomplished this, they were willing to accept the traditional roles of wife and mother. They wanted a fling. The socialist-feminists could not be satisfied with one successful love affair because their goals were much more comprehensive and consuming. Their aims were social rather than individual. Nonetheless the feminist heroine is one legitimate interpretation of the woman's dilemma in this century. Miss Glaspell, Floyd Dell, and Miss Boyce recognized that the middle-class woman was beginning to yearn for more than the traditional pattern of living. Their interpretation of her desires and ways to satisfy them was one interesting dimension to feminism.

Feminist writers took a rather different view of the bohemian feminist, whom they usually mocked. This more extreme version of feminism was not the woman lawyer or teacher but rather the woman poet, painter, or writer. She was portrayed as an aggressive young woman who knew what she wanted and where she was going. The opposite of the romantic feminist, she reversed the traditional roles in man-woman relations. The bohemian was an experimentalist, a bold practitioner of radical values. Men pleaded with her to marry them, but she refused to be tied down. As one heroine put it: "I don't want to be anybody's wife. I want to write poetry."[25] Another reprimanded her lover: "We are getting to care too much—

and you are so jealous—and there must be no more talk of marriage, for that would be very foolish."[26] A third proclaimed that she would not marry until she had "played and played and played. . . ."[27] Floyd Dell and Mary Heaton Vorse wrote some stories in the bohemian feminist vein, in which they pointed with a satirical finger to the excesses of feminism.

The men in these love relationships were invariably portrayed as weak sentimentalists while the women were rationalists. The men were romantics who believed in the mystery and beauty of love and the ethereal qualities of woman; the women, on the other hand, scoffed at these notions and talked hardheadedly of the transitory features of life and love. Bohemian feminists advocated free love while male Villagers diligently strove for marriage and permanency. Occasionally the writers allowed the man's point of view to prevail. One hero reminisced at the end of a story: "We want the old things—the best of them; things like homes, and permanence, and babies."[28] Another, talking about free love, noted that "fellows who are not in love have all kinds of batty theories. But when you care for a girl, little old City Hall is good enough for you."[29] But usually the marriage was a new kind. "Neither of us wants that—domestic atmosphere, home and all that," explained an artist in one of Neith Boyce's stories. "I should hate a woman who wanted to take care of me and make me comfortable and depend on me. Of course she has her work, and I have mine, and we can go on independently of one another."[30]

This dialogue comes close to expressing the view of some feminists toward marriage. Village feminists combined romantic and bohemian traits. Neith Boyce, for example, was a part-time bohemian; she was a writer with a husband and four children who led a traditional life in most ways, but her views toward marriage and love were radical. She once wrote Mabel Dodge Luhan, a good friend: "Both Hutch and I feel that we are free to love other people—but that nothing can break or even touch the deep vital passionate bond between *us* that exists now as it always has."[31] In another letter to Mrs. Luhan she answered the question: "Why do we want men to be monogamous?" with "Do we?—so long as they won't be, why should we want them to be? Why want anybody to be what they are not?"[32] Ida Rauh thought, "There may be some who still feel that marriage is a sacrament, but the idea is passing away."[33]

Village feminists not only wrote about free love but often practiced it. Henrietta Rodman openly lived with many men before marrying in 1913. Love affairs were considered necessary if one was to live as a sensitive human being in the Village. But these feminists were not like the fictional heroines of Neith Boyce and Floyd Dell in many other, significant ways. They were not full-time bohemians, and they never isolated themselves from the rest of society. In many activities which involved them outside of the Village, they worked with respectable people who did not look upon them as outcasts in any sense. Henrietta Rodman chose not to wear her sandals to teach at Wadleigh High School. She dressed conventionally. Living in Greenwich Village permitted these feminists greater freedom from society's watchful eye; it did not, they thought, offer a mandate for irresponsibility. In fact, they hoped to reproduce the excitement, the tolerance, and the freedom of the Village in the society at large.

None of these feminists was as emptyheaded or as unprepared for life as their romantic fictional counterparts. Nor were they unduly aggressive or mannish in the company of men. Floyd Dell considered Henrietta Rodman a lovely person, and Crystal Eastman had many male admirers. They knew what they wanted, so to speak. Yet their search was not for an identity but for a continued improvement of their life and the lives of others.

Besides romantics and bohemians, a third type of feminist was occasionally portrayed in the fiction of Susan Glaspell. This was the ultrasensitive woman, whose keen intelligence and heightened emotions led her to commit destructive acts, usually against herself. One of Miss Glaspell's heroines had an insatiable desire to create new plant forms; it was part of her urge to break every established form in nature and continuously develop new ones, and it finally led her to suicide.[34] Hutchins Hapgood has called this particular piece an example of "half mad feminism."[35] Another Glaspell heroine committed suicide to free her husband and give him the self-confidence he lacked while she lived.[36] In yet another play, a woman killed her husband because of his insensitive treatment of her.[37] In all these cases the woman protagonist found herself outraged by the circumstances of her life. She symbolized, in the extreme, the frustrated woman in American culture—a woman who could find no legitimate or peaceful means of self-expression. In desperation she turned to destruction. Miss Glaspell's suicidal heroines were the victims of a male-centured culture.

❧

Feminist writers were uniformly sympathetic to the strivings of the romantic feminist; they were playful in their handling of the bohemian feminist, for they recognized many of her idiosyncrasies and excesses in themselves and in their Village friends. Both forms of feminism (the third form being an aberration) expressed an individualistic approach to the role of woman in the modern world. As writers, Neith Boyce and Susan Glaspell interpreted the woman's problem as essentially an individual, personal one, not a social one. They empathized with the unique dilemma of their heroines and tried to express woman's lonely search for fulfillment. The focus of their romantic fiction was always personal and unique. Their answers to woman's problems—true love, diverse experiences, life as an experiment—showed their commitment to romanticism.

As theoretical activists, Henrietta Rodman and Crystal Eastman were deeply interested in changing the social fabric that stifled women. While the writers were apolitical and individualistic, Miss Eastman and Miss Rodman were visionaries who viewed woman's problem within the context of society. They did not separate the individual woman from all women, or abstract her from her environment. Rather, they concerned themselves with creating a radically new culture that would treat woman differently; in so doing, man too would be viewed in a new light. It was a far bolder, more sweeping program than that described by the feminist writers. The heroines of Susan Glaspell, Neith Boyce, and Floyd Dell may have symbolized all women, but their interpretation of woman's problem was a one-to-one affair. A reader related to the story because of the validity of the heroine's portrayal and the difficulty she faced, but the solutions remained uniquely individual.

Together, ideologists and writers presented different aspects of feminism—its individual and social natures, its cultural and individual problems, its impersonal and at the same time exceedingly personal sides. Fiction provided a neat counterpart to factual argument. Susan Glaspell's heroines added a dimension to the perplexing feelings of the modern woman which the cultural analysis of Henrietta Rodman could not provide. The humorous treatment of the bohemian feminist balanced the serious analysis of Charlotte Perkins Gilman. Village writers showed their colleagues that they must view their situation with a certain humor.

The popular view of feminism that persisted beyond 1920 was the writers' view, not the cultural analyses of Crystal Eastman or Henrietta Rodman. The dilemma of the modern woman—her search for identity and a fulfilling existence—was to be interpreted as an individual quest for romance. To this day, one of the persistent strains of feminism (noted by supporters and critics alike) is the right of a woman to be sexually free. Emancipation, feminism's major accomplishment, has not expanded woman's role or changed society from a man-centered view of the world to what Mrs. Gilman called a human-centered view. Rather, this brand of feminism has meant sexual freedom and the liberty to have an illicit love affair. The heroines of Susan Glaspell, Neith Boyce, and Floyd Dell were searching for an undefined goal; their discovery of love and romance seemed the answer, but they were not sure. Since 1920 many writers have been certain that the romantic view is the feminist view.

3

Practicing the Theory

FEMINISTS WERE interested not only in developing an ideology but in translating it into action. At first, activists such as Crystal Eastman and Henrietta Rodman worked within the existing woman's reform organization: the National American Woman Suffrage Association. In 1910 that organization was split into so many factions that propaganda work for a national woman's suffrage amendment was nil. Crystal Eastman worked with Mrs. Carrie Chapman Catt, the New York head of the group, for the passage of the suffrage law in New York State.[1] But Miss Eastman became impatient with the NAWSA's slow, laborious methods, and joined with Alice Paul in December 1912 to set up a Washington office that would lobby Congress for a federal suffrage amendment. Calling themselves the Congressional Union, these women devised

(46)

dramatic ways to capture the public's attention. Their first sensational action, in March 1913, was a march of five thousand women in Washington on the eve of Woodrow Wilson's inauguration. They followed this demonstration with a visit to the new President.[2]

Crystal Eastman worked with Alice Paul for about a year; in 1914 she was in charge of organizing local committees in the northwestern states to agitate for the vote. But her interest and participation waned. The war in Europe demanded her attention; and it became clear to her that the NAWSA was not an agency for feminist reform. For these reasons Miss Eastman became the cofounder of the New York Woman's Peace party, a group dedicated to both peace and feminism.[3] While she turned to keeping the United States out of the European war, Henrietta Rodman continued the purely feminist work of implementing Mrs. Gilman's ideology, first in New York City and then, she hoped, throughout the country. In April 1914 she organized the Feminist Alliance, an organization pledged to carry out the Gilman philosophy.

At the first meeting of the Alliance, the members issued the following declaration:

> Feminism is a movement, which demands the removal of all social, political, economic, and other discriminations which are based upon sex, and the award of all rights and duties in all fields on the basis of individual capacity alone.[4]

Composed largely of professional middle-class women and some rich society women such as Mrs. O. H. P. Belmont

and Mrs. Henry Villard, the Alliance attacked discriminatory practices toward women in specific areas. For example, a lawyers' committee was organized to ask leading
law schools to lower their barriers against women. Jessie
Ashley, a well-known attorney in the Village and cham-
pion of many Village causes, headed the committee. A
medical committee was also organized to write to the
Yale and Harvard Medical Schools.

The Feminist Alliance also criticized the fact that
American women who married foreigners lost their citi-
zenship; it urged passage of the Thompson Immigration
Bill, then before the Senate, to correct this injustice. The
Alliance also urged President Wilson to propose an
amendment providing that "no civil or political right shall
be denied to any person on account of sex."[5] It anticipated
the equal rights amendment devised by Alice Paul and
the National Woman's party in the early twenties. One
constitutional amendment, it was believed, could end all
the discriminatory laws on the state and federal books.

The personality of Henrietta Rodman dominated
the Alliance, and the group usually busied itself with her
pet projects. Since Miss Rodman was known for her
eccentricities, the schemes she advocated were certain to
be unconventional. And her interests led the group to
concentrate its energies in only one direction: Miss Rodman's campaign for a new kind of housing, especially
suited for professional working women, was the central
concern of the Alliance for many months. Using Mrs.
Gilman's theories, Miss Rodman hoped to show the world

that feminist ideology was not mere fantasy. Her utopia was to be an apartment house, equipped with a fully mechanized basement in which meals for the entire building would be prepared by professionals. The latest industrial products and principles would be utilized; the twelve-story building would provide an electric service elevator to deliver the food to each apartment. The apartments would have dull-surfaced walls to minimize cleaning chores.

Children in the apartment house would be schooled by teachers trained in the Montessori method, in a rooftop schoolroom. Mothers would be freed of what Miss Rodman called the "four primitive home industries." No longer would the professional woman have to be responsible for the "care of the children, preparation of food, care of the house, and of clothing."[6] She would be able to work at her profession during the day and be a companion to her husband in the evening. "For a man doesn't love a woman any more because she does his washing," Miss Rodman argued, "nor does it make a mother love her child any better to have to wash its face a dozen times a day."[7]

To Miss Rodman this apartment house became a necessary basis for feminine equality. It was designed specifically for the middle-class professional woman, who was Miss Rodman's ideal of the true feminist. Wealthy women who used their leisure for charity work or fashionable crusades may have supported feminism, but Miss Rodman did not consider them practicing feminists. The apartment house would answer the needs of the woman who had a productive career. By collectivizing the maintenance of the home, the professional woman could have the expert child and house care that the rich woman paid servants to perform. The house in Washington Square would offer the life of the future. It would allow women to expand their roles beyond the home, and would make it economical for more women to receive college educations and become professionals. In an interview with a *New York Times* columnist, Miss Rodman explained:

> At the present time the care of the baby is the weak point in feminism. The care of children, particularly those under four or five years of age, is the point at which feminism is most open to attack. We must have this apartment house before we can be honest feminists.[8]

To those critics who objected that the scheme removed the mother from her child, Miss Rodman responded that the woman would be providing "intelligent mothering"; this meant "an intimate spiritual relation between mother and child which enables the mother to give to the child all that she has gained from life, so that the new generation is started in advance of the old." Expert care of children could best be given by experts. Then the parents could enjoy the children together for an hour or so in the evening. Miss Rodman admitted that she did not enjoy small children herself; she found adolescents more to her liking.

Indignant traditionalists attacked Miss Rodman's plan. A woman writer responded to it in the *Times:* "We find that the secret of the feminist movement lies in a monstrous egotism, which would chain women to the oar to make money, that with that money they may buy immunity from all that is disagreeable drudgery."[9] A woman was always more effective than a man in ridiculing feminism. The anti-feminist woman proclaimed happily that women were different from men and should stay that way. Grubbing a living was the male's function; the woman ought to stay in her rightful place—the home —and not in the marketplace.

Miss Rodman's Futurist Baby-Raising Plan, as it came to be called, was described by one wry critic as a system whereby "You put the baby and the breakfast dishes on the dumbwaiter and send them down to the central kitchen-nursery-kindergarten-laundry to be cared for until needed." But *The Masses* rushed to Miss Rodman's defense. K. W. Baker, in an article for the magazine, argued that this new scheme was hardly preposterous, and cited numerous examples of negligent mothers whose children had died because of improper care. Babies who suffered "from the lack of maternal attention do not belong exclusively to emancipated mothers who have foresworn drudgery," Baker wrote. The "present methods not being quite perfect, a futurist method may conceivably be as good—or better."[10]

The Masses' support notwithstanding, Miss Rodman was called upon to defend her feminist home of the future on numerous occasions. The newspapers considered her good copy and were more than willing to give her space to elaborate what they considered her ludicrous ideas. The conservative *New York Times* reported frequently on the meetings of the Feminist Alliance and on one occasion ran a full-page feature article with a large photograph of Miss Rodman. In this article she argued that "feminism is the attempt of women to grow up, to accept the responsibilities of life, to outgrow those characteristics of childhood—selfishness and cowardliness—that we require our boys to outgrow, but that we permit and by our social system encourage our girls to retain."[11]

Throughout 1915 elaborate designs were drawn up for the apartment house by Max Heidelberg, an architect, and a site in Washington Square was chosen. Meetings were held to discuss the house's cooperative arrangements. But the scheme was temporarily abandoned for lack of finances, and the apartment house was never built. The difficulties in implementing its bold new approach to living seemed insurmountable.

More successful was the crusade of the Feminist Alliance during 1914–1915 against the New York City Board of Education, a battle inspired and initiated by Henrietta Rodman. Known as the teacher-mother controversy, it concerned the right of married women to teach, to bear children, and then to return to teaching. Clearly it was an issue that spoke directly to feminist beliefs. As an English teacher in a New York City high school, Miss Rodman had experienced discrimination firsthand. The New York City system did not like married women teaching in their schools. In fact, most school systems in the country discriminated against married teachers. In 1914 the practice was not to hire married women unless they had been separated from their husbands for at least three years or were widowed. If a woman married while teaching and became pregnant, she could not return to teach after having her child. Only three large city school systems in the country granted maternity leaves, and New York City was not one of them.[12] This policy prompted *The Masses* to write:

> The impulse of life to reproduce itself will probably not be entirely annihilated by the New York Board of Education, but we are glad to see that institution doing what it can to suppress this craze. Women teachers at least shall not be allowed leave of absence to have children.
>
> Maybe it does not come within the province of education to prevent babies from being born, but at least it makes their education unnecessary.[13]

Only single women could make good teachers, administrators thought. Married women, mothers especially, were too burdened with domestic and family chores to teach effectively. Pregnancy and the absence following the birth of the baby took the teacher away from the classroom for too long a time and thereby upset the continuity of the class. Feminists and radicals pointed out that married women made better teachers because they understood and practiced child psychology, while unmarried women were inexperienced in dealing with children. But more generally, feminists argued that no law should prevent any woman from pursuing any career she desired. Teaching, which had always been accepted as one of the few proper professions for women, ought not to be denied to married women with children.

Henrietta Rodman had married while teaching in the New York school system but had not reported that fact to the Board at the risk of losing her job. Many women followed this practice until they became pregnant, when they could no longer hide the fact. When they applied for a maternity leave it was denied, and they were suspended from their jobs. Miss Rodman never had children, but she saw this practice as a glaring example of discrimination against women. She decided to make the fight of the teacher-mothers her fight. For her, the schools' discrimination against teacher-mothers clearly demonstrated the limits society placed upon woman's development. Not being a mother herself, Miss Rodman could approach the issue on a level of philosophical principle rather than mere self-interest. Her critics could not argue that her fight was purely for personal gain.

A number of test cases on this issue were pending before the Commissioner of Education in the fall of 1914. Teachers who had been suspended for neglect of duty (because of their unauthorized maternity absence) had appealed the Board's action. Henrietta Rodman's outrage led her to organize, with the help of the Feminist Alliance, rallies to enlist support for the suspended teachers. Miss

Rodman got Charlotte Perkins Gilman to participate in the protest meetings and to accompany her when she went to appeal to Mayor Mitchel on behalf of the teachers.[14]

Floyd Dell called the Board of Education "parochial" and an "1830 Board of Education."[15] The *New York Times*, on the other hand, thought the Board was to be praised for its suspension of teacher-mothers and for having "the courage to antagonize the sentimentalists. . . ."[16] In a novel interpretation, the *Times* saw the advocates of teacher-mothers as sentimentalists; the feminists were traditionalists, the *Times* argued, in their insistence that teacher-mothers were better equipped than single women to deal with children. The *Times* did not address itself to the other feminist contention, namely, that a teacher-mother had a right to a professional career, too.

As the Feminist Alliance agitation continued, including public meetings and demonstrations in front of the Mayor's office and the verbal support of such distinguished men as John Dewey and Rabbi Stephen Wise, the Mayor urged compromise. Board members were uncertain; they did not like being pressured. But one member offered a plan by which a teacher could leave teaching during the fifth month of pregnancy and return eighteen months after the child was born, providing she passed a physical examination.[17] Although radical feminists considered this policy unsatisfactory because the leave period was too long, it marked the first acknowledgment by the

New York Board of Education that it employed married women who could become mothers.

With a moderate solution in sight, the drama moved to a new level of interest when Miss Rodman was suspended. On November 10, 1914, she had written a letter to the sports columnist of the *New York Tribune,* suggesting that he go see a game called "mother baiting." It was a new kind of game whose object was "to kick the mothers out of their positions in the public schools. It will be played according to the rules of the Board of Education." She went on to describe the game as being very popular with the majority of the Board. "The game is rather rough, but, like wifebeating, which used to be so popular, it's always played for the good of the women."[18] This irreverent description infuriated the staid Board members so that they charged Miss Rodman with gross misconduct and insubordination and suspended her for the rest of the school year.

"I am sorry if in writing that letter I overstepped the bounds of what is proper in a fair fight," Miss Rodman commented after her suspension. But, she went on, working for a public institution did not deprive one of his constitutional liberties.

> In all the ten years of my service in the public schools I have met with little but punishment. So I am not surprised, but I considered your action unjust. In my work I considered that I have been bullied, insulted, and robbed of money and credit

by the Board of Education and its subordinates. In all this time I have never fought the board on a personal issue, or one in which my personal interests were at stake.[19]

When questioned directly by Board President Thomas W. Churchill as to what she meant by saying she had been robbed, Miss Rodman replied that she was referring to her salary—it was lower than that of male teachers. According to the *Tribune*, Churchill walked away from the feminist teacher white with rage while Miss Rodman left in tears.

To her feminist supporters Henrietta Rodman was now a martyr. As the main speaker at meeting after meeting, she proclaimed the injustice of her suspension. Her fight, she insisted, was different from that of teacher-mothers. Their cases "involve the question whether married teachers shall have the right to have children. My case involved my right to be a citizen as well as a teacher."[20] Rather than argue the strictly feminist line— that she had been discriminated against because she was a woman—Miss Rodman contended that she had been deprived of her civil liberties. The principle of free speech and freedom of dissent for a government employee thus became the basis of the fight. Strategically, this took the discussion out of the realm of woman's suffrage and emancipation, and made it not a sex issue but a human issue. Philosophically, of course, this fit nicely with feminist thinking. As Mrs. Gilman and Miss Rodman had said repeatedly, the goal of women was to be complete human beings. The issue of free speech was a crucial one in a humane society.

After Miss Rodman's arraignment, the Board appointed a committee of investigation. Gilbert E. Roe, the noted attorney who defended many feminists and radicals, represented Miss Rodman at the closed door session which was to rule on her suspension. In a statement to the press before the final decision, Miss Rodman said, "I believe that it is very dangerous to American institutions, and altogether contrary to American ideals of liberty and justice, that a citizen can be suspended from his position without pay because he has made a criticism of a public board."[21] Despite her protests, she was suspended without pay for another eight months, until September 1, 1915. In an effort to be moderate, the Board changed the charge to read "insubordination" and not "insubordination and gross misconduct." In her remarks after the decision was announced, Miss Rodman commented: "My suspension amounts to a fine of $1800 for writing a satirical letter about the Board of Education's mother-teacher question which in ten years from now will be universally regarded as immoral and absurd."[22]

The crusade to eliminate discrimination against teacher-mothers now took on a new fervor. The Teachers League of New York City voted to reimburse Miss Rodman, while Mrs. O. H. P. Belmont called a special meeting to raise money for her.[23] Teachers considered forming a union which could strike in retaliation to the Board's unjust policies. At a socialist rally a few months later, Miss Rodman decried the continued abuses suffered by married teachers.[24] This energetic outpouring of feminist indignation forced a special committee of the Board to recommend a two-year maternity leave for married teachers. And the Commission of Education reinstated seventeen teacher-mothers with full pay for their suspended time.

Miss Rodman did not personally benefit from this changed policy, but she rejoiced in her comrades' success. "This will affect the curriculum in every school, for mothers have a more practical outlook of life than unmarried women and know better what the children in the schools need." The decision would also help women achieve the equality that was deservedly theirs: "Women teachers will have intellectual growth with their emotional development, and they will cease to be the one-sided beings most women in the world of necessity have been."[25]

During the spring of 1915 Miss Rodman appealed her suspension, only to have it denied. She criticized the two-year leave period as being unduly long, and she continued to point out the Board's discriminatory practices. In June she was transferred to the Julia Richman High School—a form of punishment, she thought.[26]

With the end of the school year in June 1915, the controversy died away. The feminists had won a modest victory; New York City became the fourth city in the country to permit maternity leaves of absence; and the next year Henrietta Rodman returned to teach without a flurry of dissension or publicity. She was not able to interest her followers in further action against discrimination in the educational system. After the war she organized a teachers union; but during the war years the influx of women into the work force probably contributed to a more sympathetic attitude toward all working women, teacher-mothers included. The need for teachers as well as the relaxed policy toward maternity leaves dissipated the strength of the feminist argument.

Miss Rodman enjoyed the support of the liberal press in her fight with the Board of Education. The *New Republic*, for instance, asked in an editorial relating to the free-speech issue of Miss Rodman's case: "How far should persons be compelled to give up their rights as citizens when they enter the public service?"[27] And a year after the controversy, a prominent educational journal referred to the Rodman case as an example of injustice.[28] Miss Rodman's limited victory did not discourage her, but rather indicated that the traditional system was both penetrable and changeable. She continued to battle for the feminist cause.

At times her buoyant and enthusiastic commitment to feminism took on a carefree note. In December 1914, for example, she organized the Feminist Alliance's first costume ball. It was a gala Greenwich Village affair. The major theme was woman's dress from primitive to futuristic times. Although no trousers showed up, Miss Rodman's adopted daughter wore knickerbockers. According to the *Times* reporter, she "looked like a pretty boy with her short cropped hair, loose blouse, golf stockings, and sandals." Miss Rodman, who came in classical dress, was reported as saying that the ideal feminine dress was the Chinese woman's outfit of loose trousers and a long coat to the knees.[29] Freedom and new styles of life for women, according to Henrietta Rodman, meant the freedom to dress comfortably, live in comfortable dwellings, and work when and where one liked. The *joie de vivre* of the Feminist Alliance's first costume ball was a symbol of the new feminist society.

❧

Apart from the Feminist Alliance, most Greenwich Village feminists joined together informally to work for whatever issue seemed crucial at the moment. Birth control was one. It embodied so many of the beliefs of the Village community that they all enthusiastically supported it. Birth control was thought to be essential to woman's emancipation; the betterment of the working-man's lot depended upon it; and the preservation of human integrity demanded that information on family planning be available to anyone who wanted it. These beliefs were shared by feminists, socialists, anarchists, and labor leaders. To Village socialists, the monopoly of birth-control information by the rich was symptomatic of the class deceit inherent in capitalism. The rich man and woman knew about contraception and practiced it, but they piously refused the same information to the poor.

In 1873 Anthony Comstock and his Society for the

Suppression of Vice had successfully agitated for a federal law that banned the sale or distribution through the mail of contraceptive information or devices. Section 211 of the U.S. Criminal Code, which embodied the law, had been generally ignored when the information was discreetly mailed or sold. Middle- and upper-class men found condoms available for purchase, and middle-class women knew about various douches, powders, and pessaries. But poor working-class women did not. They neither understood when conception occurred (as a matter of fact, neither did most men, women, and gynecologists[30]) or how to prevent it. Margaret Sanger, a trained nurse, had been beseeched by poor women on the Lower East Side of New York to tell them how to prevent having more babies. They were worn out by frequent childbearing and -rearing. Mrs. Sanger did not know the answer to their questions in 1912, but she resolved to find out.

After Mrs. Sanger began studying the subject, she started a magazine, the *Woman Rebel*, in March 1914, to give working women information about birth control. It was an issue of this magazine that got her in trouble with authorities and resulted in a grand jury indictment on nine counts of alleged violation of the federal statute. Rather than face a long jail sentence, she decided to leave the country. While in England she studied all the information she could get on birth control, became friends with Havelock Ellis, and upon her return dedicated herself to spreading the birth-control message throughout the United States. In October 1916 she opened the first birth-control clinic in America. As she later wrote, "The most

far-reaching social development of modern times is the
revolt of woman against sex servitude."[31] Only when
women controlled their bodies, Mrs. Sanger argued, would
they be truly free. She dedicated the next several decades
to fulfilling her pledge.[32]

Other members of the Village community spoke
out on the subject of birth control. Max Eastman, from
his position as editor of *The Masses*, wrote editorials in
which he argued that birth control was as essential to
woman's emancipation as suffrage was. He considered
birth control part of the social revolution that was trans-
forming the world. Using the ideas of Robert Owen and
James Mill as his philosophical foundation, Eastman saw
a direct connection between limiting the population and
ameliorating the worker's living conditions. Not only
would wages increase as the number of workers decreased,
but, more significant, "an unskilled worker with a large
family of half-starving children *cannot even* fight for freedom."[33] Every rational person should know that "it would
be the heart of moral wisdom that the bearing and rearing
of children should always be a deliberate and therefore responsible act."[34]

The Masses raised money for Margaret Sanger and
her husband when the two were arrested for distributing
birth-control pamphlets. They reported the events of
William Sanger's trial as well as of his wife's efforts. Max
Eastman often raised the issue of freedom as it related to
distributing birth-control information.[35] He ridiculed
those who would suppress its dissemination.

Emma Goldman became *The Masses'* real heroine

in this struggle. Miss Goldman, a well-known anarchist, had been preaching birth control for a decade. She displayed the dogged militancy that appealed to Eastman and his feminist friends; Mrs. Sanger was sometimes too moderate for their tastes. When Emma Goldman was sentenced to fifteen days in jail for delivering a lecture on birth control, *The Masses* printed her defense. It reminded its readers that although Miss Goldman had made this same speech on numerous occasions, it was not until the reactionary New York City police heard it that she was arrested. Emma Goldman's eloquent defense warmed the hearts of radicals:

> Your Honor: If giving one's life for the purpose of awakening race consciousness in the masses, and consciousness which will impel them to bring quality and not quantity into society, if that be a crime, I am glad to be such a criminal.

Later in her testimony Miss Goldman summarized the feminist position: "After all, the question of birth control is largely a workingman's question, above all a working woman's question."[36]

The Masses editors suggested that Miss Goldman had been arrested because of her political radicalism, not her activities on behalf of birth control. By June 1916 birth control had received so much publicity that the police had stopped arresting distributors of the forbidden pamphlets. According to *The Masses*, only socialists, anarchists, and other radicals were being pinched. The obscenity statute, under which the arrests were made, had a catch-all clause which allowed the police to arrest anyone they considered undesirable. Most prosecuting attorneys admitted by 1916 that the statute was unworkable; but when an admitted anarchist such as Emma Goldman allegedly incited the people to radical action, on whatever subject, the statute was conveniently used to arrest her.

In March 1916 Henrietta Rodman was writing to her friends and asking them to work with her for an amendment to the New York Penal Code "to permit duly licensed physicians to prescribe methods of preventing conception."[37] At a birth-control meeting in Carnegie Hall in the summer of 1916, a large audience voiced their disapproval of the obscenity statute; the district attorney of New York was quoted as saying he would not arrest anyone distributing birth-control pamphlets "providing the law is broken decently."[38] What did that mean? *The Masses* wondered.

Feminists found themselves personally involved in the controversy when Ida Rauh Eastman, Max Eastman's wife, was arrested in Union Square for distributing birth-control pamphlets. According to Miss Rauh's own account, she initiated the legal hassle because she believed that the inhibiting law would be corrected only after it had been tested in court. Thus she and a friend, attorney Jessie Ashley, borrowed a chauffeured limousine and went to Union Square to distribute the pamphlets—with a great deal of flourish so as to insure their arrest.[39] They did.

Miss Rauh and Miss Ashley were arrested, charged with a misdemeanor, and released on bail. Miss Ashley had her trial first and received a ten-day jail sentence and a $50 fine. Miss Rauh's trial took place a year and a half later and was dismissed.[40]

While the birth-control issue was still alive during the summer of 1916, *The Masses* made much of the fact that the obscenity law had been applied in a discriminatory manner. Rose Pastor Stokes, a woman of working-class origins who had married a socialist millionaire, had distributed birth-control pamphlets along with Ida Rauh, but she had not been arrested. *The Masses* concluded that Miss Rauh was arrested because she wanted "longshoremen and washerwomen to know about it,"[41] while Mrs. Stokes's action went unpunished because of her class position. *The Masses* writers were convinced that a conspiracy of silence prevented birth-control information from reaching the working class, and that rich women, even those with good radical credentials, would not suffer the consequences of their actions because their class protected them.

Jessie Ashley called her efforts with Ida Rauh "a strictly illegal success."[42] By January 1917 the public seemed tired of the numerous arrests, and willing to accept minimum and discreet public discussion of the subject. The Women's City Club of New York held meetings to discuss birth control, and most people seemed to feel that if the information were distributed without fanfare, no one would object. Still, feminists looked forward to a serious revision of the obscenity law so that, in the words of Miss Ashley, "Perhaps it may soon be a crime in the eyes of the law to have too many children, just as it is a crime in the eyes of humanity now."[43]

Although the battle in the streets was over, feminists continued to propagandize for a more enlightened attitude toward marrige and family planning generally. Floyd Dell, who was also an editor for *The Masses*, wrote a pamphlet on the subject for the American Birth Control League. Called "The Outline of Marriage," it reflected the feminist philosophy of family planning as well as the larger issue of value reorientation. In a brisk, humorous style Dell presented the views of an ordinary couple named Myrtle and George alongside the views of a biologist and an anthropologist. Each described, from his own perspective, what marriage in the modern world meant. The evidence led clearly to one conclusion: marriage ought to be based upon love and companionship. Children, as Myrtle said in the fictional interview, should be "something else for us to share together." The experts agreed with this ordinary couple; the biologist demonstrated in his presentation that reproduction was a distinct and separate act from lovemaking. The anthropologist described primitive cultures in which the male dominated and the female was relegated to childbearing functions only. The point was that in a modern, industrial culture, where advanced knowledge of biology and psychology was available, men and women ought to share equally in the joys of life.

Dell, an enthusiastic feminist, continued this line of reasoning by calling those past cultures in which the male dominated, "homosexual." He thought this type of culture should be replaced rapidly with a modern, heterosexual culture. Birth control was only one element in the new mixture that was essential for happiness in the twentieth century.[44] But its acceptance would bring American culture one step closer to complete democratization. Typical of his feminist colleagues, Dell tried, through his writings, to chip away at the status quo at the same time he described what the new society would be like. Each victory, he believed, however modest, brought the millennium closer.

Because feminists had a constant vision, they could be enthusiastic about specific causes which they knew were part of their larger goal. Because they had a utopian dream of an egalitarian society based upon their feminist ideology, they could battle the New York Board of Education, devise schemes for suitable homes for professional women, and march with Margaret Sanger. In their everyday lives they were doing what their ideology demanded of them: they were trying to remake society. Women such as Henrietta Rodman were committed to the long struggle. Unfortunately for them, most people did not (and do not) devote themselves to reform causes over a long period of time. Activism ultimately wanes, especially if victory is ephemeral or out of sight. Feminists continually reminded their followers that the end was no less than the total reconstruction of society—an honest but not especially comforting appraisal.

❦ 4 ❦

Feminist Organizations, Village Style

The Masses and the Provincetown Players, an unusual Village theatrical group, were used by Village feminists as sounding boards for ideas and as channels for communicating views and plans. In many ways these atypical organizations contributed to an always evolving feminist ideology. Being intellectuals, feminists spent almost as much time writing and talking about their ideas as they did doing something about them. They saw themselves as both articulators and actors in the feminist cause. Groups devoted to discussing, describing, and understanding feminism were as crucial to feminists as organizations such as the Feminist Alliance, which was devoted to specific progaganda, educational, and legislative action.

The Masses and the Provincetown Players were Village institutions. Staffed by Villagers, they quite appropriately reflected the favorite concerns of the inhabitants. Many Village feminists were board members and contributors to both ventures. A homey, in-group atmosphere prevailed in the offices of *The Masses* and in the little theater on MacDougal Street. Although neither organization occupied all the energies of the feminists—with the exception of Susan Glaspell, who devoted herself completely to the Provincetown Players—they offered them amusing and constructive outlets for their thoughts. The Villagers often found it more pleasant to exchange ideas with their friends than to try to educate the general public.

These outlets for feminist expression were unique for several reasons. For one thing, men and women feminists worked together in them in harmony. By contrast, the traditional nineteenth-century woman reformer had been anti-male. Elizabeth Cady Stanton, one of the pillars of the woman's suffrage movement, had openly declared that men were the natural enemies of the suffragists. Henry Blackwell, a male suffragist, had a difficult time convincing his suffragist wife Lucy Stone that having men in the suffrage organization would help its cause.[1] But the Village feminist had no feelings of sex antagonism. Henrietta Rodman, Crystal Eastman, Ida Rauh, and all of their feminist friends worked with men in the Village, and gaily welcomed their help. In fact, they frequently found the male feminists to be more ardent than some of their women supporters. After all, such men as Max Eastman and Floyd Dell had developed serious philosophical principles of feminism. They did not rely solely upon slogans or even upon the views of Charlotte Perkins-Gilman. Dell, for example, devised an elaborate explanation for the cause of the woman's revolt and the beginnings of the feminist movement.[2]

The Masses and the Provincetown Players were also unique in being individualistic enterprises within social frameworks. Because the Villagers valued individual expression and freedom, they liked organizations that allowed for diversity and variation. Being democratic socialists as well as feminists, they wanted their social organizations to implement their beliefs. Thus *The Masses* was cooperatively owned, and all its contributing editors participated in decision-making. They thrashed out their differences of opinion until they decided the contents of each issue. The same thing happened at the Provincetown Theater. Each meeting of the executive board of the Provincetown Players was devoted to a lengthy discussion of the proposed next play. No decision was made individually. The fierce individualist might express himself, but ultimately the individual will was joined with others to effect a decision. This process created tremendous organizational problems for both groups. Not only was it inefficient for authority to be so loosely assigned, but feuds and resentments ultimately led to the disintegration of the cooperative ideal.

Neither group could be called activist. Although

The Masses purported to reach large numbers of people, its audience was actually quite limited. The Provincetown Players, by definition an experimental group, was established strictly for entertainment. When it stopped being an amusing experience for the Villagers, they abandoned it.

Neither of these institutions was self-perpetuating. The publishing career of *The Masses* was ended in November 1917 when the Post Office censored it for "seditious" anti-war propaganda, and the editors were ordered to stop publishing. When Max Eastman resumed publishing under a new title, *The Liberator*, the content of the magazine was largely political and geared to lauding the new Russia. The Provincetown Players lost their vitality during 1917 and 1918 when the United States entered the war and a new group of Villagers, more interested in commercial theater, took over. By 1920 neither *The Masses* nor the Provincetown Players functioned as they had during the previous decade, and feminism lost its Village support.

But while both groups were alive they offered the feminists vital support. *The Masses*, especially, articulated the male feminist point of view and confirmed the women feminists' position. To analyze the writing in *The Masses* on feminism is to see its similarities with and differences from the feminist ideology of Crystal Eastman and Henrietta Rodman. Under the editorship of Max Eastman, from December 1912 until its demise, feminism was one of *The Masses'* major causes. It was one of the "isms" which, to paraphrase Art Young, *The Masses'* great political cartoonist, gave a "reasonable hope of improving, however little, the happiness and character of human beings in the mass."[3] *The Masses* advocated feminism because women were one of the most neglected groups in society. As Villagers, *Masses* editors and writers were exposed to many models of the feminist: Max Eastman's wife, Ida Rauh; Max's sister, Crystal Eastman; Henrietta Rodman; and writer Mary Heaton Vorse, who was on *The Masses'* editorial board. These women provided them with daily examples of what woman could achieve in the modern world, and reinforced their eagerness to write about the evil society that inhibited woman's development. The pages of the magazine were filled with stories and pictures satirizing the reactionary society that refused to recognize the legitimate rights of women.

Max Eastman's commitment to feminism was already evident in 1909 when he organized the first Men's League for Woman Suffrage. This seemed like a natural enterprise for Eastman, since his mother and sister were avid suffragists. He followed their lead and astonished himself by becoming a popular speaker and writer for the cause. "I should certainly not have chosen to get my first taste of fame as a suffrage orator,"[4] he later wrote, but such was his fate. "There was nothing harder for a man with my mamma's boy complex to do than stand up and be counted as a male suffragette. It meant not only that I had asserted my manhood, but that I had passed beyond the need of asserting it." Eastman also contended that feminists were "different from mere reformers—they're the people that want to live."[5]

When he was asked to become the editor of *The Masses* without pay, Eastman hesitatingly accepted. Floyd Dell became his associate editor a year later. Together they confirmed the magazine's commitment to feminism. Dell has been described as the man who "expressed the spirit of the self-conscious woman of the time: the woman who accepts herself without the conventional lies thrust upon her by man's ancient imagination."[6] He thought of himself as an artist rather than a political propagandist, and wrote uncounted pieces on the emancipation of women. He also reviewed the latest books on feminism and sexology. His intense interest in the role of women was bound up with his fascination for the subject of love and happiness in the modern world.

Dell was a romantic who pursued true love ferociously in the 1910's. When he came to Greenwich Village in 1913 from Chicago, he had already had one unsuccessful marriage and a number of ephemeral love affairs. In the Village he hoped to find, personally and philosophically, the fulfillment of his romantic search. Dell argued that free love was as essential to the life of the artist in twentieth-century America as it had been to the old world poet. The artist, by definition, needed freedom and openness. Marriage could never be a desirable life pattern for him. In an industrial culture, where capitalism always kept the artist poor, Dell considered marriage even more repressive. A poet, he contended, could not marry because it would mean "childbearing for her and wife support for me."[7] Dell's frequent and articulate statements of his beliefs made him one of the most vigorous male feminists in the Village. Dell used every opportunity to write on this subject for *The Masses*. He wanted to see woman emancipated so that she could be self-supporting; this would in turn emancipate man, who was traditionally chained to the moneymaking machine. When both were able to earn a living, a man and a woman could live together without economic strings attached.[8] Dell believed that intelligent people should have the freedom to enter into a love relationship or terminate it at will. Such an agreement was essential for human fulfillment. It was also imperative in a modern capitalistic society in which the high cost of living made marriage prohibitive. Because women would have children, in or out of wedlock, mothers and children ought to be protected by law regardless of the circumstances under which the woman became a mother. The only agency capable of supporting a family, according to Dell, was the state.

Only when women had economic independence and free unions were recognized as proper, Dell thought, could love be fulfilling and complete. Modern man needed educating in the ways of true, deep love, and Dell hoped that modern woman could teach him.[9]

So long as any woman is denied the right to her own life and happiness, no man has a right to his; and every man who walks freely in his man's world, walks on an iron floor, whereunder, bound and flung into her dungeon lies a woman-slave.[10]

This plaint is typical of Dell's romantic, often emotional, tone. Woman and the machine were the two great forces in the world; which would triumph he could not say. Will women, he asked, rise above their narrow individualism and fulfill their potentialities? He hoped so.[11]

Dell tried to evolve a systematic theory of woman in the modern industrial world. His conviction that woman's dilemma was a crucial part of the disjointedness of contemporary living became the basis for his elaborate explanation of the modern condition. Weaving together many of the threads that had appeared in his writings in *The Masses* as well as his later work, he synthesized an analysis of the feminist revolt. His anthropological approach, similar to Charlotte Perkins Gilman's, was contained in *Love in the Machine Age*.[12] In the book Dell described the pre-industrial agrarian world in which a patriarchal structure had prevailed. The father had dominated in this culture by arranging the marriages of his sons and perpetuating the belief in male superiority. Adultery was permitted as was homosexuality. Because property was all-important and the father determined how his property would be distributed, his sons were totally dependent upon him—until they married and became fathers with sons they could dominate.

This family structure and value system had been

carried on into the industrial age, Dell claimed, but were obsolete. Sexually, emotionally, and in every other way, the patriarchal culture was wrong for the industrial world. In order to create a value system consonant with the industrial order, the first, most pressing need was to remove the archaic values of the pre-industrial system. A serious appraisal must then be made of capitalism and the love relationship. Dell thought woman's emancipation was conceived under capitalism. The idea originated with man's awareness of the economic difficulties of life under capitalism. An ordinary man, as well as an artist, had a hard time earning a living and thus could not afford a wife and children. Women would have to work, men concluded, in order to make survival possible. But once woman grasped the idea of independence, she turned her "secret discontent into overt rebellion.[13]

This bleak portrait of the struggle for existence under capitalism led Floyd Dell to other conclusions: the need for birth control and free love as the only feasible ways of achieving love, and the need for a complete re-evaluation of sex. "Capitalism," he argued, "had deprived us of the opportunity for responsible fatherhood, and it compelled upon the young woman who preferred our society an indecent choice between childlessness and something too much resembling martyrdom."[14] With the new knowledge available about physiology, all the outmoded notions about sex and reproduction could be abandoned. The modern understanding of bodily functions "had laid the basis for a successful feminist movement."[15] Men and women now had the information to enable them to live without false taboos. Sexual fulfillment could be realized without shame or risk. Family planning could, and should, be practiced.

In all, Dell saw woman's problem as part of the larger cultural dilemma. Although they had unique problems, women shared with men a desire to right the terrible wrongs of the industrial order. In a thoughtful piece reflecting upon his theories, Dell concluded: "The woman's revolt took its place in our imagination as a part of the industrial revolution. They were oppressed; so was mankind at large."[16] In the twentieth century both women and men, using new knowledge, could live freely. The Village community, by practicing the new doctrines, could lead all Americans into a new and fuller life.

Max Eastman shared many of Dell's ideas about feminism, but he couched his views within a liberal democratic framework. He argued that suffrage was the first step to freedom. A woman ought to be allowed to choose her way of life; men should not dictate the choice, and domesticity should not be forced upon a woman. "There are many women who, on account of their natural disposition perhaps, or perhaps on account of their social or financial situation, can not function happily in that sphere."[17] Political and social inequality must be eliminated first.

Eastman thought universal education came next. Like Henrietta Rodman and Crystal Eastman, he believed that the woman who was sheltered in the home was often not fit "to bring children into this world"; she needed to know "to the full the rough actual character of the world into which she is bringing them."[18] Her fulfillment depended on her familiarity with every part of the world's life: marketplace, home, school, and church.

Both Eastman and Floyd Dell showed the influence of Charlotte Perkins Gilman in their programs: political equality through the vote, together with economic liberation and improved educational opportunities, would make woman a whole human being. Dell and Eastman, like Mrs. Gilman and Henrietta Rodman, acknowledged that women in their present state were inferior to men—but the inferiority was cultural, not biological. When women were given the cultural advantages that men naturally enjoyed, they would become equal. Traditional attitudes toward women were culturally determined, therefore culturally changeable.

Changes in the law, such as an amendment giving women the vote, would lead to changes in attitudes. Allowing women to attend universities in greater number, for example, would inevitably bring a radical change in values. Men and traditional women would accept woman's new roles once she had been provided the material opportunity. When Dell and Eastman imagined the kind of society that would result from this total equality of opportunity, they could see state nurseries for the care of children, professional women in every field, birth control and family planning, and permissive love arrangements (where compatibility determined the permanence of the relationship). Once the legislative and political changes had been made, the utopia would be won without revolution.

Many leading feminists appreciated *The Masses'* crusading zeal on their behalf. Five Village feminists placed an advertisement in the February 1916 issue asking women readers to donate $5 or more as a New Year's gift to the magazine. "Max Eastman, Floyd Dell, Art Young, and the rest are genuine warmhearted Feminists. They like us and want us to win." The advertisement also set down some of the goals which the feminists shared with their favorite magazine: "When we fight for suffrage, for economic freedom, for professional opportunities, for scientific sex knowledge, there stands *The Masses*, always understanding, always helping."[19]

In its literary crusade for feminism, *The Masses* often concentrated on specific evils which feminism and socialism would remedy. For example, prostitution was a result of the capitalist system. All women, according to *The Masses*, were victims: in sexual relations they bore children and the burden of raising them; in economic relations they were dependents, never knowing whether they would have adequate finances to support the family. But the prostitute was the inevitable, extreme victim of the exploitative capitalist system, the product of commercial greed and avarice. Eliminating prostitution depended upon the overthrow of the existing economic system.

Max Eastman showed in an editorial how difficult it was for a working girl to earn a respectable living. The industrialists' huge profits denied the ordinary human being, and especially the vulnerable woman, a decent livelihood. In an accompanying cartoon by Art Young, a huge dog labeled "Commercial Greed" lapped up everything in sight; behind the dog was a discarded woman's hat and the word "Prostitution."[20]

The prostitute was also sympathetically drawn in *The Masses'* fiction. "She is cursed and hounded and mulcted and jailed," one story said, "for earning her livelihood by the only means she knows." The author wondered "if God loves her the less for this."[21] Surely she was the rejected member of society, the woman who was nobody's sister.

"How many of you went into this life because you could not make enough money to live?" asked Reverend Paul Smith at a meeting reported in *The Masses*. All of the two hundred prostitutes in the hall raised their hands. As their leader told the clergyman, in terms which the editors would have used under similar circumstances: "You don't do any good by attacking us. Why don't you attack those conditions?"[22] No woman wanted to sell herself to a man; but inequitable capitalism, with the owners exploiting their workers, made it impossible for a woman to earn a decent, honorable living. True to its feminist-socialist views, *The Masses* argued that if material conditions could be changed, behavior patterns would also change.

The sexual double standard and the larger problem of love in the modern world were favorite topics of *The*

Masses. Why should a man be able to have extramarital relations while a woman could not? Why should fidelity be only a female virtue? Why should marriage be the enslavement it had become in American society? Some of *The Masses'* writers thought true love within marriage impossible. Charles W. Wood, a regular contributor, called New York a city of five million people whose principal industry was keeping the sexes apart. "Marriage is prohibited by the high cost of living. Free love is prohibited by common consent. Slave love, the only other kind of love known to modern science, is prohibited by statute. . . ."[23]

The antiquated divorce laws of New York State were also an object for attack. The laws chained women to men and to lives they abhorred. Cartoons and articles frequently portrayed men as ignorant, drunken, and cruel while women were selfless and long suffering. The intransigence of the capitalist system, the hypocrisy of values, and the sham of marriage were vividly and repeatedly described. These frequent discussions of woman's dilemma demonstrated the centrality of this subject in the thinking of *The Masses* staff. It also gave feminists the lurid details they needed to support their views.

Sometimes *The Masses* offered scientific data to substantiate its faith in feminism. Floyd Dell reviewed a study of Dr. Leta Hollingworth, for example, which proved, much to his own surprise and delight, that females were biologically capable of being just as intellectually creative as men. Through a careful study of babies, Dr.

Hollingworth found no perceptible difference in the anatomical variability of males and females. This meant that women were as variable by nature as men were, and could therefore be as creative. Another of Dr. Hollingworth's studies demonstrated that women, counter to public opinion, were not unreliable or inefficient during their menstrual period. Using twenty-three women and two men as her sampling, the doctor proved that women were as capable of doing any task that men could do.[24]

Floyd Dell had to admit that even many male feminists had not believed in woman's diversity and in her creative abilities. They had championed woman's freedom but had never thought it could offer the total equality that Dr. Hollingworth suggested. Now Dell's and all male feminists' greatest hopes were fulfilled: woman could truly be man's equal in every area of human endeavor. It took only Dr. Hollingworth's scientific evidence to convince Dell of a position he had held in faith for many years.

The Masses and its editors shared with their women feminist friends an understanding of feminism in broad cultural terms. Although Floyd Dell's writing often focused on the possibilities of love in an industrial culture, he saw feminism in the context of the total culture's value system. All feminists analyzed the relationship of values, role expectations, and economic conditions to the larger society and found their contemporary culture wanting. Yet all believed in attacking specific social ills and reforming the society part by part. They preached about the ideal culture while directing their energies to attacking narrow, concrete problems. Male feminists buttressed the judgments of their women friends. Their conviction of the rightness of feminism made it more difficult for the skeptics to denounce feminism as the whim of eccentric ladies.

Even after World War I began, *The Masses* continued to devote considerable space to the feminist cause. But as the possibility grew of American entry into the war, the magazine became filled with anti-war cartoons and essays. Max Eastman considered the woman's peace movement as one of the few lights in a darkening sky. He pleaded with the women of America to work against American entry into the war and to join with the women of the world in a peace effort. There could be no progress toward women's rights during wartime, or in a reactionary country or world. Thus the need for a speedy end to the war and the continued neutrality of the United States.[25] Feminism must be tied to pacifism in the emergency. If women were not pacifists, who would be? *The Masses* reported at length the activities of the women's peace organizations and advised all feminists to become pacifists. When *The Masses* closed down in November 1917, the political atmosphere was no longer right for a serious continuation of the feminist debate or a dispassionate consideration of pacifism.

❧

Of the several qualities of the Villager in the 1910's, none was rarer than his ability to view himself in perspective, and his sense of humor. He could be engaged as well as detached from his efforts. Floyd Dell could write a serious study of feminism and then write a comedy on the same subject. Max Eastman could earnestly advocate woman's suffrage and then spoof it on the stage. Some of the Villagers, of course, were deadly serious about their crusades; Henrietta Rodman called a special meeting of the Liberal Club after a performance of Floyd Dell's *What Eight Million Women Want* to discuss his comical treatment of woman's suffrage.[26] But most Villagers took it more lightly. They respected the seriousness of their feminist beliefs at the same time they appreciated the excesses they sometimes committed in behalf of their views. Fortunately they had an arena in which they could express both feelings.

"We had no mission. We just had plays—and we had fun."[27] So Mary Heaton Vorse explained what the Provincetown Players was all about. The Players was the Village's mirror: a place to test serious, innovative drama but, more important, also a place for Villagers to poke fun at their latest social theories. Experimental and entertaining, it was more often the latter. Being a unique Village creation, it was developed to satisfy the creating group. The world that was criticized in the Provincetown Theater was often not the alien outside world but the Village world. It was also a world created during wartime, when the Villagers tried to make "a social effort to live again—spiritually, to recover from discouragement and disappointment, to be free of the poison of self and the poison of the world."[28]

(85)

There were precedents for this adventure. Henrietta Rodman's Liberal Club Theater and the Washington Square Players were little-theater groups which had performed in the Village since 1912. One critic has written that these two groups emanating from the Liberal Club "changed the entire character of the American theatre. . . ."[29] In any event, these early dramatic groups gave the Village community the acting, writing, and directing experience it later used in the Provincetown Theater. Floyd Dell's comedies had been the mainstay of the Liberal Club Theater. Henrietta Rodman cajoled him into writing a play for the theater the first day he arrived in the Village in 1913. For the next two years he virtually ran the whole operation: "I had been playwright, stage designer, scene painter, stage manager and actor."[30] Ida Rauh, Max Eastman's wife, acted and directed in plays for the Washington Square Players, and Susan Glaspell wrote for the same group.

What better way, thought the Villagers, to test new ideas, spoof old ones, and ham it up for your friends than to start a little theater? Disgusted with Broadway commercialism, George Cram Cook and Susan Glaspell wrote a play called *Suppressed Desires* for the Washington Square Players. When this group thought the play too esoteric for its tastes, the Cooks decided to stage it themselves. That summer, 1915, they gathered their Village friends together in Mary Heaton Vorse's wharf house in Provincetown, Massachusetts, and produced their first play. It was the inauspicious beginning of the Provincetown Players.[31] Being intellectuals, they hastily wrote a constitution and formulated the rules by which they would govern themselves. The revolutionary journalist John Reed wrote the resolution: "It is the primary object of the Provincetown Players to encourage the writing of American plays of real artistic, literary and dramatic—as opposed to Broadway—merit."[32]

The Villagers supported this new theater group with enthusiasm. Max Eastman helped John Reed write its constitution; Ida Rauh became its leading actress; Bobby Jones created stage settings; Mary Heaton Vorse contributed her wharf house for its original location; and Susan Glaspell, George Cram Cook, Floyd Dell, Neith Boyce, and Hutchins Hapgood wrote plays for it. It was to be a truly Village enterprise with no thought of commercial acceptance or success. And, as befitted all good socialistic enterprises, it was to be cooperatively run. No professionals would be allowed in, and every writer, actor, poet, and teacher in the group would have to work to maintain his active membership.

In its first few seasons the Provincetown Players had spirit and energy to compensate for their amateurishness. The Villagers participated in the summer seasons and then, beginning in the fall of 1916, in the winter seasons held in the Village. Moving into rather primitive quarters next door to the Liberal Club, the Provincetown Players borrowed the portable stage equipment of the Club and prepared for their New York opening. Rough benches and the unkempt hall helped to make the audience think they were seeing a new form of drama. To the Villagers this theater was an outlet for excitement, not a total commitment. To John Reed it was an entertaining and creative experience which he could indulge in between reporting assignments. To Max Eastman it was an amusing opportunity to act and relax; and to Ida Rauh it was an exhilarating experience to discover that acting was a truly fulfilling activity.[33] To Floyd Dell it was a chance to write satire and to be bored while watching someone else's effort.[34]

George Cram Cook, the primary mover of the Provincetown group, was the most devoted of its members. He had come to New York with his new wife, Susan Glaspell, in 1913 and was looking for a job. Earning a living had never come easy for him, but the Provincetown Theater became his full-time interest and love. All his energies went to making it the most innovative theater in the world. Although his spirit was infectious, he was never able to elicit the response he desired. At best the Provincetown Players produced amusing plays, usually feminist spoofs, for a Village audience.

The plays borrowed heavily from Village gossip and Village controversies. The theater often became a nighttime debating ground for the argument that began earlier in the day at the Liberal Club. References to Village life were sprinkled throughout the plays to amuse the audience. In one play, for example, the feminist's enthusiasm (most probably Henrietta Rodman's) for Freudianism was spoofed. Neith Boyce's first play was about the

(88)

"stormy loves of Mabel Dodge and Jack Reed."[35] Miss Boyce and her husband, Hutchins Hapgood, wrote a play called *Enemies* that was a satirical dialogue based upon a discussion they had had at home. Susan Glaspell's *The People* was about a radical magazine that appeared to be *The Masses.* Not all the plays were direct representations of Village personalities, but many of the most popular ones were.

The two most prolific writers for the group were Susan Glaspell and Floyd Dell. Dell's comedies were among the most popular offerings. His protagonists were, true to his feminist philosophy, always women. The type of woman varied—fickle, flighty, intellectual. His themes were "love, the conditions of staying in love, and . . . the temptations of new loves."[36] Dell knew that he liked to romanticize woman and to be optimistic about her future. Thus he often used his comedies to correct his own excesses. As he himself explained, "I live, then and always, naively, earnestly, hopefully, believing that I had solved or was about to solve the riddle of how to be happy and stay happy in love; but the mocking imp that popped up in my mind and wrote these comedies, saw all my weaknesses."[37]

The feminist whom Dell admired and whose cause he espoused in the pages of *The Masses* was often the object of satire in his plays. Her intellectuality became coldness and ultrarationality. She was articulate but aggressive, levelheaded and pragmatic—a set of traits which, ironically, often led her to unhappiness. As one intellectual heroine stated, "I know exactly what I want, and it doesn't include being disowned by my family and having my picture in the morning newspaper. Free love? Not at all. I want to be married."[38] But this heroine failed because of her cold, practical nature. Her self-assurance would not allow her to be swept off her feet, and the result of her makeup was failure in love.

Floyd Dell's one-sided women could not have it both ways; intellectual women were unhappy in love while feminine and emotional women were emptyheaded. His flighty heroines usually personified the best and worst in the myth of womanhood. They were mysterious, divine, and elusive; they were also unpredictable and irrational. They wanted to teach their socialist lovers how to dance and be in love, not knowing precisely what love meant. Dell amused himself by using his heroines as models for the conservative man's view of women. One of Dell's disillusioned men characterized woman as "an inferior being, with a weak body, a stunted mind, devoid of creative power. . . ." Her utter hopelessness, which Dell enjoyed dramatizing in the extreme, made her "a being who does not know how to work, nor how to talk, nor even how to play!"[39]

In satirizing the conservative's exaggerated notions of woman's weaknesses as well as the strengths of the emancipated woman, Dell dramatized the comic results of his honesty. Human jealousy and rage were part of life in the Village as in the larger society. The traditional bourgeois household was filled with hypocrisies and comic follies, but so was the Village household. The perfect love relationship with an enlightened new woman and new man was not yet to be found in either life.

Susan Glaspell's comedies were thematically like Dell's. In *Woman's Honor* she satirized both the outmoded male code of honor as well as the "modern" woman. The plot concerned a murder suspect who refused to tell where he was on the night of the crime because he had been with a married woman; rather than tarnish her reputation, he was willing to go to prison for a crime he had not committed. To compound this comic situation, Miss Glaspell presented an assortment of neurotic women who came to his defense once the newspapers publicized his reason for silence. An excessively motherly woman, a scornful woman, a silly, romantic woman, and a shielded woman appeared, all claiming to be the woman the suspect was with on the night of the murder. Their reasons for coming to his defense revealed their own inadequacies. When all of them quarreled to decide who should stay and help the innocent victim, the suspect proclaimed in dismay, "Oh hell, I'll plead guilty."[40]

Susan Glaspell's dramas, on the other hand, tried to cope with the feminist in tragic and heroic terms. Her view was usually pessimistic. The intelligent, sensitive woman, her favorite tragic figure, was driven to suicide because she could not abide the pressures of modern living. Miss Glaspell's heroines often seemed tortured, unbalanced, and near madness. In one play an ordinary farm wife killed her husband because of his inhuman treatment of

(91)

her. All women seemed tainted and unsuited to modern life; the mysterious malady struck the simple farm wife as well as the intellectually sophisticated woman. As one woman says to another in one of the plays: "We all go through the same things—it's all just a different kind of the same thing."[41] Men did not know this intuitive understanding that all women had, nor the unspeakable misery of womanhood. This idea of a bond among all women was peculiar to romantic feminists. At the same time they claimed to be like men in every important way, the romantics spoke mystically and eloquently of woman's sense.

Most of the plays of the Provincetown Players were forgotten the day after the run ended. But a few of the plays, and some of the participants, achieved national fame. Eugene O'Neill began his playwriting career with the Players, and in the early 1920's achieved his first great success, *The Emperor Jones*. Of the Village group, Susan Glaspell and Ida Rauh gained reputations. Ludwig Lewisohn, drama critic for *The Nation*, considered one of Miss Glaspell's plays, *Bernice*, "not only her masterpiece but one of the indisputably important dramas of the modern English or American theater. . . ."[42] *Suppressed Desires*, by Miss Glaspell and her husband, became a favorite one-act play which has been included in numerous collections. Mary Heaton Vorse thought Miss Glaspell a "natural" playwright.[43] Many critics considered her plays in the same rank with Eugene O'Neill's.

Ida Rauh became known as the "Duse of Mac-

Dougal Street" or, as one writer called her, "An Experimental Bernhardt."[44] She was the star of the Provincetown Players and symbolized the whole dramatic venture: a talented woman who had turned to acting for its experimental opportunities. Miss Rauh, one report said, "has been a sculptress, lawyer, poetess, and social reformer, and brings keen intelligence to the interpretation of her parts."[45] Although she never ventured beyond the Provincetown Theater, she attracted the attention of actors such as Charlie Chaplin, who came to the Village to see her performances.[46] This success surprised Miss Rauh, as she did not consider herself an actress and did not seek professional recognition. Fame pleased her, but she always remembered that she was in it for fun.

Generally the performances of the Provincetown Players were uneven, often inept and amateurish. Ludwig Lewisohn panned the Players as being "without energy, without freshness, without the natural stir and eloquence that come from within."[47] And Floyd Dell confessed that "nothing was too mad or silly to do in the Provincetown Theatre, and I suffered some of the most excruciating hours of painful and exasperated boredom there as a member of the audience that I have ever experienced in my life."[48] The Provincetown Players were not designed to please large and diverse audiences, but Dell did not seem to think they amused the Villagers either. When the amusement value was lost to many of the Village feminists, they dropped out of active participation in the theater.

(93)

George Cram Cook became disillusioned with the group when they began courting the favor of audiences rather than concentrating on new and unusual drama. By 1920 the serious-minded Cook and his lighthearted friends abandoned the venture, leaving the management of the theater to professionals. Neith Boyce later recalled how devoted Cook was to the theater.

> He worked fanatically as men worked only for an idea, molding and using that group as he worked rebellious clay. Then when success came in money and public notice, talk of a bigger theatre and of going uptown, Jig said this: "What we need is a smaller theatre."[49]

Cook's goals were too far-reaching to appeal to fun-loving Villagers or commercially minded theater people. His search for new dramatic forms, which often took the shape of obscure, mystical dramas, was uncongenial to the thinking of professionals who wanted large audiences. Thus an adventure which appealed to the dramatic and energetic spirits of Ida Rauh, John Reed, Neith Boyce, and Floyd Dell ended in disappointment for some and indifference for most.

The coming of the war could not help but contribute to the downfall of the original Provincetown Players. The public mood could no longer sustain a light attitude toward social problems. Villagers turned from satirical comedies to peace progaganda. John Reed was busy reporting the Bolshevik Revolution; Max and Crystal

Eastman were involved in pacifist organizations; and Floyd Dell was writing anti-war pieces for *The Masses*. When professionals took over the Provincetown Players, they made the theater a full-time serious business.

❧

By 1920 Village feminists found themselves without Village organizations to articulate their views. The Feminist Alliance of Henrietta Rodman had disappeared when its leader became a spokesman for such leading radicals as Morris Hillquit and Elizabeth Gurley Flynn. The Alliance had never had a working structure anyway, so when its dynamic leader switched to other concerns, the organization dissolved. Woman suffrage groups were congratulating themselves on their victory and retiring from feminist action. *The Masses* had been replaced by *The Liberator* and was dealing in strictly political propaganda. The Provincetown Players had become a commercial theater. The feminist ideology no longer grew and developed new and different interpretations of modern woman's dilemma. The whole subject was put aside, and feminists lost even their limited audience.

❧ 5 ❧

The Challenge of War

THE LINK between feminism and pacifism seemed to some feminists to be a natural one. Women produce life, nurture their offspring, and are emotionally involved in perpetuating rather than destroying life. Nineteenth-century suffragists such as Julia Ward Howe had declared that "Peace and woman suffrage go together, masculine government being founded upon the predominance of physical force." But however much these suffragists preached pacifism, they never practiced it. Their twentieth-century counterparts who claimed to be pacifists "served their country first and their principles afterwards."[1] Feminist-pacifists in the Village, however, stuck to their principles. Crystal Eastman became the major spokesman and activist for the feminist-pacifist position. She considered pacifism a fundamental principle of life.

The pacifist's function, she wrote, "is to establish new values, to create an overpowering sense of the sacredness of life, so that war will be unthinkable."[2] In other words, the task was identical to the feminist's: to reforge society so that new values could become the basis of human relations.

As an articulate, thoughtful intellectual, Crystal Eastman sought to explain the relationship of pacifism to feminism. In a pamphlet written for the Woman's Peace party, she explained how a feminist could justify joining an exclusively woman's organization. Did not such a group reflect the older suffragist view of sex antagonism? "Is peace any more a concern of women than of men?" Miss Eastman asked. "Is it not of universal human concern?"

> For a feminist—one who believes in breaking down sex barriers so that women and men can work and play and build the world together—it is not an easy question to answer. Yet the answer when I finally worked it out in my own mind, convinced me that we should be proud and glad, even as feminists, to work for the Woman's Peace Party.

The Woman's Peace party, she continued, represented the first serious attempt to organize the world for peace. This "unique tradition" would be lost if the party merged with the international revolutionary movement. Further, the women of New York, who had just won the vote in 1918, had been "born into a world at war"; this fact would shape their political thinking and behavior. As women pacifists they could "dedicate their new political power, not to local reforms or personal ambitions, not to discovering the differences between the Democratic and Republican parties, but to *ridding the world of war*."[3]

Hoping to use the WPP as a political party (what the suffragist Alice Paul had hoped to do with the suffrage party), Crystal Eastman thought women could and would vote for peace. By insuring a peaceful society, women could then create the feminist society they wanted. The vote gave women the power to achieve equality through peaceable and legislative means. Since women naturally hated war, as Miss Eastman and her colleagues argued, they would naturally vote against war.

All feminists believed that women had a *natural* aversion to war. This is curious, since feminists argued on other occasions that there were no such things as natural feminine instincts; the only differences between men and women, according to Mrs. Gilman and her followers, were cultural differences. Crystal Eastman slipped out of this intellectual inconsistency by agreeing that men hated war as much as women did; but men had voted for war—now women, with their newly acquired political power, were going to bail men out of the mess they had created. Her views were shared by other feminist-pacifists. "As women," read the preamble of the Woman's Peace party, "we are especially the custodians of the life of the ages."

> Equally with men pacifists, we understand that planned-for, legalized, wholesale, human slaughter

is the sum of all villainies. As women, we feel a peculiar moral passion of revolt against both the cruelty and waste of war.[4]

The explicit reference to male pacifists was another tactic of the feminist-pacifists. They acknowledged that some men were right-thinking, but thought most men unfortunately accepted war as part of the natural order.

Of all their causes, feminists were the most sex-conscious about pacifism. "The one small green leaf left on the withered tree of internationalism by the spring of 1915," declared Mary Heaton Vorse, "was the woman's movement."[5] When Mrs. Vorse, a Village feminist, reported on the war from France in 1917, she quoted extensively from a friend in Paris named Madame Etienne, who epitomized woman's attitude toward war. This Frenchwoman, who had lost three sons in the war, explained that "As long as men love war like that, there will be war, and when they hate it as we hate it, there will be no more war." Mrs. Vorse thought that the strange gulf she had felt during the war between men and women was caused precisely by the fact that birth was woman's most intense experience, while men's "intensest moment is when they are called on by war to go out and destroy the lives for which we have risked our own."[6]

Mabel Dodge, another feminist who was in Europe when war broke out, noted how patriotism mesmerized the soldiers into killing and other acts of violence. Only when she talked to women about the war was she able to communicate her distress. The men did not understand her horror of war. Her visit convinced her that the "only hope of permanent peace lies in a woman's war against war."[7] Joseph O'Brien, Mary Heaton Vorse's husband, echoed the feminist sentiment when he argued that "Man is the homicidal sex; he has the psychological need to kill which has been strengthened rather than diminished by centuries of conduct indefensible on any ground save force."[8] All the writings of the feminist-pacifists repeated this theme.

Pacifism is as radical a goal as feminism, for it too requires a drastic alteration of fundamental attitudes. In 1914 most Americans claimed to be peaceloving and believed, with President Wilson, that the European war did not concern them. From August 1914 until April 1917, they watched the hostilities anxiously. When Wilson declared war on Germany in April 1917, Americans dutifully prepared for it. Their pacifism gave way in the face of foreign danger. Crystal Eastman, like other dedicated pacifists, met frustration at every turn. But Miss Eastman's commitment to the ideals of a liberal democracy never wavered. The dilemma of the cultural reformer, whether feminist or pacifist, was heightened during wartime. Crystal Eastman believed that the liberal means available in a representative democracy could achieve the radical ends she sought. She was wrong. A close look at her peace work is instructive on this point.

Miss Eastman became the prime mover in two pacifist organizations: throughout 1915 she presided over the Woman's Peace party of New York,[9] and in 1916 she became executive secretary of the American Union Against Militarism. While the WPP had only female members, the Union boasted a membership of prominent men and women pacifists. Oswald Garrison Villard, editor and publisher of *The Nation*, Paul Kellogg, editor of *Survey*, Max Eastman, and Lillian Wald, head of the Henry Street Settlement House, were on the Union's board of directors. In her work for both organizations, Miss Eastman displayed considerable talent as a public relations agent. True to the democratic tradition, she believed that an informed public would act "properly" when presented with necessary information—and, more significant, she expected the government to respond to the people's will. *Four Lights*, the pamphlet of the New York WPP, used the format and many of the writers of *The Masses*. It reflected the woman's point of view on the war, on the need for a social revolution, and on the ways to win world peace. The artist Boardman Robinson drew for *Four Lights*, and Howard Brubaker and Max Eastman wrote articles for it. Robinson's drawing of a woman wearing black, with the caption, "You Are the Widows of Democracy," effectively portrayed the feminist view of World War I.[10]

Four Lights had a brief life. 1917, the year it began, was not an especially good one for radical journals that claimed that pro-German meant "One who believes in democracy and peace and is opposed to all forms of imperialism and conquest." Or that military training, at a time when the United States had just passed a universal military training bill, was "training in automatic animal obedience. It is a cunning destroyer of personal independence and free judgment."[11] Or that a woman's way (once America had entered the war) was to train her sons for violence and fighting so they would be prepared. The woman who suggested this also noted that "it takes but a minute to destroy a boy into whose making have gone eighteen years of thoughtful care."[12] The government confiscated the issues of *Four Lights* that contained these interpretations, and in October 1917 it forced the publication to cease.

Before this happened, the editors of *Four Lights* tried to rebut the charge that they were pro-German. They did this by publishing a genealogy of their contributors and pointing out that fifteen of the twenty-eight editors were eligible for the Daughters of the American Revolution.[13] This was small consolation for the authorities, who suppressed the magazine nonetheless. The WPP found itself open to grave suspicion, too. Comic accusations under normal conditions were serious indictments in 1917.

Four Lights' focus on internationalism reflected the new concern of radical feminist-pacifists. Crystal Eastman and others saw peace and woman's role as world-wide problems requiring world-wide attention. "We burn to pledge our country for World Union as the only hope of both peace and democracy," wrote the editors of *Four Lights*. After the success of the Bolshevik Revolution they proclaimed: "We hail the Russian Revolution with mad glad joy."[14] Only international plans for peace, they thought, would prevent future wars.

Four Lights also shared Crystal Eastman's conviction that women who had the vote would never vote for war; therefore women's political freedom would make the world permanently peaceful. In Australia, where women had the vote, the electorate had turned down a conscription law in February 1917. Proud feminist-pacifists saw this victory as clearly the result of the woman's vote, and so did Anna Howard Shaw, past president of the Woman's Suffrage party.[15] But while the Reverend Shaw had faith, the radical pacifists continued their propaganda. Women might be more peaceloving than men, but they had to be educated to the ways of the world and trained to use the vote.

In addition to *Four Lights*, Crystal Eastman used some new and different methods to fight the preparedness legislation pending in Congress in 1915, and to bring the peace message before the American people. In November 1915 she executed what she called "the best woman's stunt I have ever seen pulled off."[16] With $10,000 donated by Mrs. Henry Ford, the WPP sent 8,942 telegrams to important women throughout the country urging them to wire President Wilson to press for negotiations with Germany. Jane Addams had signed all the telegrams, and the women responded in great numbers. Within twenty-four hours the White House received a thousand messages. Early in 1916, Crystal Eastman appeared in a

Paramount film, *Shall We Prepare?*, in which she called the government rearmament program a step toward war rather than insurance for peace.[17] With the aid of her husband, the artist Walter Fuller, Miss Eastman organized a gigantic "War Against War" exhibit in April 1916. It opened at 368 Fulton Street in New York on April 13, and included huge models of all the evil means of destruction—an armoured dinosaur, the latest dreadnought, modern guns, and so forth—to demonstrate the terror of war. According to the WPP, eight thousand people a day saw the free exhibit.

Meanwhile Miss Eastman spoke on such subjects as the League of Nations, the need for a negotiated peace, and the reasons why the United States should stay out of the war. J. Salwyn Schapiro of Columbia University wrote to her: "You have become a sort of walking 'Forum' and from what I hear you are doing excellent work. Much better, isn't it, to settle the affairs of nations than to broil a chop?"[18] After April 1917, however, it was more difficult for Miss Eastman to gain a public forum. The WPP was forced to sponsor secretly a lecture series in December 1917, for fear that its public advocacy would bring reprisal. At one of the lectures, Miss Eastman rose from the audience and revealed to her listeners the sponsorship of the Woman's Peace party of New York. She assured them that the WPP had never "in the slightest degree counseled resistance to the selective service law nor any other policy of obstruction." She used the opportunity to advocate a peace conference that would truly represent the people's will, universal disarmament, and the League of Nations. Always the teacher, she asked her listeners:

> On the basis of that record we ask protection from the government for our propaganda no matter how popular it may become. We ask tolerance from those who think our ideas are wrong; and from those who think our ideas are fundamentally sound, whether they agreed with us about the necessity of entering the war or not, we ask friendship and loyalty and support.[19]

The peace movement gave Miss Eastman the chance to speak of the ideological problems of American and world culture, too. She pleaded for a peace that would be fundamentally different from the old industrial, male-centered society. Urging the creation of a new internationalism, in 1918 she declared: "Crying 'peace' in these days will not shorten the war, but crying 'internationalism' may."[20]

When Mrs. Whitehouse, executive secretary of the Woman's Suffrage party, pledged her 500,000 members to support the government in case of war, Crystal Eastman showed little tolerance. She wrote to a follower: "I believe a great many suffragists, who are not pacifists, felt decidedly aggrieved that their services had been so lightly pledged to a government which has denied to them for forty years a fundamental democratic right."[21] Consistent suffragists, Miss Eastman believed, should have demanded their rights before supporting the war effort.

When the Bolshevik Revolution took Russia out of the war, Crystal Eastman watched events there with excitement and hope. In America, meanwhile, she continued to support socialist candidates such as New York's mayoral candidate, Morris Hillquit. In one speech she said "President Wilson may learn a lesson" if Hillquit were elected. She was shouted down before she finished.[22] In February 1918 she sent a message to the All Russian Congress of Peasants' Soviets congratulating them on their courage and expressing her support for their new government. She hoped she could help to bring about official recognition of the boleshevik government in the United States.[23] Miss Eastman believed that Russia had, in fact, achieved the new world, and in her zeal for the Soviet experiment she organized mass meetings to advocate recognition.

Critics of the pacifists and bolsheviks now labeled the Woman's Peace party pro-communist. Margaret Lane, executive secretary and a loyal defender of Miss Eastman, denied newspaper accounts of WPP meetings:

> We held the meeting primarily for liberals and the audience was made up chiefly of that group of people. I personally asked the two or three people who entered wearing a red button or flag if they would mind removing them so that there might be no cause for disturbance, which they did.[24]

Despite Mrs. Lane's explanations, the Woman's Peace party took a decidedly leftward turn under Miss

Eastman's prodding. Her devotion to communist Russia resulted in the loss of valued party members. Mrs. Agnes Leach, the former treasurer and a long-time friend of the organization, resigned from the executive board because of the WPP's new radical direction. Mrs. Henry Villard, another faithful advocate, ended her participation in April 1919 because of the new international outlook of the organization—"She disapproved of Crystal and her enthusiasm for Lenin," wrote the new chairman.[25] The old guard feminist-pacifists were leaving the Woman's Peace party, which had been renamed the Women's International League for Peace and Freedom, and were being replaced by young political radicals whose interest in peace was coupled with internationalism.

Another critic of the New York branch of the Woman's Peace party was the national chairman of the organization, Jane Addams. Miss Addams considered Crystal Eastman's New York chapter too radical and intemperate. In the winter of 1917, for example, Miss Addams refused to speak at a large public dinner sponsored by the New York group, saying, "I am rather sceptical as to the value of public meetings on peace just now."[26] But in private correspondence with her friend Lillian Wald (who worked with Crystal Eastman in the American Union Against Militarism), Miss Addams expressed misgivings about Miss Eastman herself.[27] And Miss Wald, like Jane Addams a pacifist who reluctantly supported the war, wrote her friend President Wilson of her support for his war declaration:

Perhaps fighting is the only public service our nation is up to rendering. That is a hard saying. But it is what I have been thinking, since I listened to the ignoble speeches of the majority of those who had been accredited as our Representatives in Congress, and when I added these to the discord of hostility which greeted your appeal on January 22nd for a world order based on justice. Out of sin and suffering, then, may our nation be led into the paths of service which alone are freedom and peace. May God enable you even now to lead the nation in his ways. There are fateful choices still in your hands. Be our leader once again, Mr. President.[28]

Crystal Eastman could not accept Miss Wald's romantic liberal view of the war. She could never say, "Out of sin and suffering, then, may our nation be led into the paths of service which alone are freedom and peace." She had no faith, as liberals did, that suffering was purification and travail the basis for goodness. The radical had to create a better world out of the materials available. But sharing both the pragmatism and the methodology of the liberals, Miss Eastman wrote, in June 1917, that although the Union had been opposed to the declaration of war, they held "a stake in the outcome of it." Therefore they wished to see an American victory—a victory along the humane, international lines outlined by the President.

This was to become Crystal Eastman's enduring

theme until the end of the war: America should win "not by entangling alliances with the spirit of revenge and lust for conquest which inspire some of the old world governments with which she is allied," but by the general peace terms suggested by the bolsheviks: no forcible annexations, no punitive indemnities, and free development of all nationalities.[29] Constructive pacifism during wartime, Miss Eastman thought, meant the creation of viable peace negotiations. Her advocacy of the bolshevik peace plan, though radical, was quite acceptable to Lillian Wald and other liberals who sought a speedy negotiated peace. Miss Eastman's propaganda program seemed to them a workable one. It also gave them something to do.

But the liberal-radical coalition within the Union gradually disintegrated, as had the alliance within the WPP. One significant dispute that found Lillian Wald and Crystal Eastman on opposite sides was the relationship to the People's Council, a radical peace group which held its first meeting in Minneapolis in September 1917. Miss Eastman had helped to organize the council, a popular movement with its greatest appeal to socialist and leftist labor groups, and wanted to send Union representatives to its first meeting. Lillian Wald considered it an "impulsive" organization while the Union stood for "reflective thought of those opposed to war."[30] She thought the People's Council was "an outlet to the radical sentiment" and resisted association with it.[31] A power struggle ensued and Miss Eastman won an empty victory: the board voted to send representatives, but the chairman

(Miss Wald), vice-chairman, and two influential board members voted against it. Norman Thomas and L. Hollingsworth Wood, chosen to represent the Union at the meeting, never attended because of "unavoidable necessity."[32]

By November 1917 Crystal Eastman had become discouraged with peace work during wartime. She found the American peace movement hopelessly torn apart. "The American Union Committee could do very little in an organized public way," she told a committee meeting, "in the present state of public feeling and under the existing limitations upon freedom of discussion."[33] Lillian Wald wrote privately to Jane Addams, expressing her disappointment with Crystal Eastman's judgment: "There are many other things that I must plead for that I feel that I could not throw away any part of my reputation for good judgment. I am sure that a committee of liberals is needed and if it is not the American Union it must be some other union."[34] Frustration and disillusion characterized the feelings of both women.

Crystal Eastman's sense of hopelessness was so strong that she resigned from the American Union Against Militarism.[35] "I am perfectly sure," she wrote to Oswald Garrison Villard, "that I could never say I believe in a vigorous prosecution of the war." Not being ready to die for the cause for which American boys were dying, she could not recommend support of the war effort to anyone else. "Further, I can see that with this point of view our chances of leading a great movement in wartime are very slight."[36] Writing to Jane Addams of her decision, she confessed: "My whole philosophy about the way to get things done has undergone a change in the last two or three weeks and I suppose that it is inevitably somehow reflected in the fortunes of the American Union."[37]

Curiously, Crystal Eastman did not consider herself a radical activist. She thought only an activist could exist in group efforts during a war. Not being one, she planned to turn to writing.[38] Miss Eastman's dilemma was the dilemma of a theoretical radical in a liberal skin. To Lillian Wald, for example, Crystal Eastman *was* a radical because of her impatience and dogmatic temperament. She spoke like one as well. Yet Miss Eastman viewed herself as a moderate who would never resort to drastic or unlawful means to accomplish her ends. She could never become wholly involved in radical peace groups such as the People's Council. After April 1917 her unique and effective relationship with liberals became exceedingly difficult. She became, by November 1917, a pacifist who had lost her moorings.

After her resignation from the American Union, Miss Eastman became co-editor with her brother Max of *The Liberator*. She continued her peace work in the Woman's Peace party, a group that was temperamentally and philosophically more suited to her needs. Lillian Wald, on the other hand, left the peace movement altogether, though she still believed that all voices ought to be heard. In June 1918, for example, she asked Professor Felix Adler to use his influence in Washington so that

Crystal Eastman might speak on behalf of her brother Max and *The Masses* (which was being withheld from the newsstands as allegedly subversive in content). "In these troubled times," Miss Wald wrote, "it seems to me of vital importance that the radical element that is back of the President should not be estranged and that they should be free to exercise their influence in the support of government."[39]

Perhaps in her personal dilemma Crystal Eastman reflected the real alienation of the intellectual in wartime. As a socialist she had a comprehensive explanation for the causes of war; as a humane pacifist she believed in non-violent means to attain her utopia. This combination allowed her to work with liberals before American entry into the war. After that, even such basic liberal beliefs as free speech were stifled; and, ironically, the radical Miss Eastman fought for those classic liberal doctrines on which liberals were now silent. Most liberals and pacifists suspended their ideology to join the war effort. Radical pacifists who openly resisted the government's war policies were persecuted and prosecuted for their actions. Those few radicals, such as Crystal Eastman, who had no temperament for direct-action techniques, were left in limbo.

So were Miss Eastman's Village friends. When *The Masses* was forced to stop printing in November 1917, Max Eastman, Floyd Dell, and Art Young, the editors, were tried for publishing a seditious magazine. Ultimately they were acquitted, but Max Eastman complained that "you can't even collect your thoughts without getting arrested for unlawful assemblage."[40] His friend John Reed expressed the outrage of the dissenter during wartime:

> Now these stupid and oppressive people must learn that "free speech" must be free—even if unpleasant. They must learn, if they don't want to be taught by bloody rebellion, that the thought and feeling of mankind will and shall be expressed.[41]

The degree of loyalty demanded by the government was often ludicrous. Oswald Garrison Villard, editor of the *New York Evening Post* and an ardent pacifist, was asked to resign from the presidency of the Philharmonic Society because, as one director put it, "pacifism and music would not mix in war time."[42]

The Village community split over this general issue. All supported the right of an individual to free speech, but many believed that self-restraint was proper in wartime and that a radical ought not embarrass the government or obstruct the war effort. Crystal Eastman, her brother Max, Ida Rauh, Henrietta Rodman, and most of *The Masses* staff waged an active fight for civil liberties. As Miss Eastman said, "It takes an exceedingly large-minded liberal to fight for the right of another man to say exactly what he himself does not want said."[43] She knew that all warring countries demanded efficiency at home in order to wage a successful war, and that they often sacrificed their citizens' freedoms to expediency.

At the end of the war, Crystal Eastman's thoughts

returned to feminism. Her last major effort for the Women's International League reflected her desire to turn the woman's organization into a feminist one. She organized its second annual convention in March 1919 and called it the "Woman's Freedom Congress." What would be woman's new opportunities and problems in 1919? the conference program asked. What effect would woman's participation in the war effort have on her life in peacetime? Miss Eastman invited many of New York City's leading feminists to speak, including Henrietta Rodman, Ida Rauh, and Jane Addams.[44]

We have no record of these speeches, though the convention was apparently a success. Yet the League's board of directors did not feel that a feminist program was a legitimate part of their peace platform. When they refused to act upon Miss Eastman's suggestions, she turned to other interests. She visited Europe in the spring of 1919, and her observation of the communist revolution in Hungary confirmed her belief in the validity of socialism. She returned to the United States more convinced than ever that socialism and feminism were workable, interconnected systems.

Still, while she approved of revolutionary change abroad, she continued to advocate evolutionary reform at home. Her talent for translating broad goals into specific objectives was nowhere better illustrated than in the program she devised for the restructuring of values along feminist lines, which she presented to Alice Paul, her old friend and in 1920 the head of the Woman's party. Miss

Eastman hoped that the Woman's party, now that they had won the vote, would consider a feminist program at their annual meeting in 1921. Her program included:

> Having achieved political liberty for women this organization pledges itself to make an end to the subjection of women in all its remaining forms. Among our tasks we emphasize these:
>
> 1. To remove all barriers of law or custom or regulation which prevent women from holding public office—the highest as well as the lowest—from entering into and succeeding in any profession, from going into or getting on in any business, from practicing any trade or joining the union of her trade.
>
> 2. So to remake the marriage laws and so to modify public opinion that the status of the woman whose chosen work in home-making shall no longer be that of the dependent entitled to her board and keep in return for her services, but that of a full partner.
>
> 3. To rid the country of all laws which deny women access to scientific information concerning the limitation of families.
>
> 4. To re-write the laws of divorce, of inheritance, of the guardianship of children, and the laws for the regulation of sexual morality and disease, on a basis of equality. . . .
>
> 5. To legitimatize all children.

6. To establish a liberal endowment of motherhood.

None of these proposals was new. Feminists had advocated such reforms for ten years without success. Surely, Miss Eastman thought, after a bloody war the suffragists would see to the constructive reordering of society along feminist lines. Surely Alice Paul, the radical suffragist, would adopt the feminist program as her own. But Miss Paul answered, "Yes, I believe in all these things, but I am not interested in writing a fine program. I am interested in getting something done." "That is the way," Miss Eastman remarked, "she takes the wind out of your sails."

Alice Paul had concentrated all of her efforts upon securing the vote, but Miss Eastman thought she had lost sight of larger feminist goals. "The world war meant no moment's wavering in her purpose," Miss Eastman wrote, "in fact she *used* the war with serene audacity to further her purpose."[45] Thus the vote had been won, the suffrage movement was over; but the feminist campaign that should have begun did not. Alice Paul's National Woman's party decided to concentrate all its energies on an equal rights amendment, and one-tenth of the membership of NAWSA regrouped to become the League of Women Voters. Miss Paul changed her narrow focus upon suffrage to an equally narrow focus upon the equal rights amendment. She argued, as suffragists had for more than fifty years, that the amendment would alter the dimen-

sions of women's lives. Except for one disastrous foray
into partisan politics in 1920, the League of Women
Voters spent its energy educating women in political mat-
ters and studiously avoided discussions of specifically
feminist demands. The Women's International League
for Peace and Freedom propagandized for peace, and
there remained no Village institution to carry the banner
of feminism. For emancipated flappers, it was a matter of
no concern. After all, they *were* free. Crystal Eastman's
pacifist crusade had won neither a revitalized feminism
nor an enlightened peace.

❧ 6 ❧

The New Woman?

AFTER 1920 the literary feminists continued to write but never enjoyed their earlier popularity. Susan Glaspell spent the early years of the twenties in Greece with her husband George Cram Cook. For Cook, Greece was the fulfillment of a life's dream. He learned Greek and became a philosopher-peasant. When he died suddenly in 1924, Miss Glaspell returned to the United States to write his life story, *The Road to the Temple*. She also resumed her novel writing, which she had ignored during her years with the Provincetown Players. But her novels in the 1920's and 1930's were romantic, sentimental, and melodramatic. They lacked the social bite or awareness of her earlier work.[1] The new woman, whom she had described so well during the 1910's, was no longer considered an exciting subject. Miss Glaspell's romanticism, which appealed to an earlier generation, seemed dated. Her play *Alison's House*, however, won the Pulitzer Prize in 1931. Thereafter, though she continued to publish, her audience was modest. During the New Deal era, under the auspices of the Works Progress Administration, she became the director of the Midwest Play Bureau for the Federal Theaters.[2] She died in 1948.

Neith Boyce, who lived until 1951, wrote only occasionally after the war. Her oldest son, Boyce, had died at the age of seventeen in 1919, and this tragedy caused her great and continuous suffering. The Village community, which had so often been the catalyst for her writing (for example, her plays for the Provincetown Players), was gone. She wrote a short story infrequently and a long autobiography that was never published. *Harry*, a short book about her son, had a small printing. Her correspondence with Mabel Dodge Luhan indicates that Neith Boyce never lost her interest in life; but she no longer sought outward means of expression or recognition. During the twenties she wrote to Mrs. Luhan:

> I live in a world where neither happiness nor unhappiness have any place—Joy has a place—and pain—they are to me *both* positive realities—But this world is a magnificent one—it overwhelms me by its vastness, its splendor, its *heroic* quality—all its lines and colors are on a vast and brilliant scale—it takes effort to live in it—effort that often leaves me flat and crushed—but it is the only place I *can* live in now—[3]

Ida Rauh is now the only woman survivor of the Village group. But her active involvement in social causes and feminism ended in 1920. She moved to Taos, New

Mexico, in the twenties with her son, Daniel Eastman, for
health reasons. Although she remained interested in social
issues, no movement enlisted her. A short book of her
poetry was published in 1959.[4] She now lives in Greenwich Village, not far from her old neighborhood. But
today the hotel in which she lives is owned by New York
University and is a dormitory for its men students, except
for a few apartments for such old-time residents as Miss
Rauh. She exhibits the same vitality today that characterized her group of social feminists fifty years ago.

Henrietta Rodman continued to crusade for radical
causes after the war, and especially for reforms in the
Board of Education. She worked for the formation of a
teacher's union and was denied a loyalty certificate in
1922 when it was demanded of every teacher. Opposing
the Lusk Law, which required every teacher to take a
loyalty oath, she refused to appear before the advisory
committee to answer questions concerning her beliefs. In
December 1922 she was stricken with a complete paralysis
of her right side. Surgery for the removal of a cerebral
tumor was unsuccessful, and she died on March 21, 1923.
She was forty-five years old.[5]

After the war, Crystal Eastman spent all her time
writing and editing. Her feminist program had found no
supporters. She dismissed Alice Paul as being "sex-
conscious but not class-conscious."[6] In writing about the
exciting revolutions in Russia and Hungary, she hoped to
participate in the great changes that she thought were
reshaping the world. When her brother Max and Floyd

Dell launched *The Liberator*, Crystal Eastman became a co-editor of this new radical magazine. Its goal was to express the new freedom that the Bolshevik Revolution was bringing to the world. *The Liberator* was not to be cooperatively owned as *The Masses* had been. Rather, Max and Crystal Eastman would jointly own it and would then be free to say "what they truly think."[7] Many of *The Masses'* contributing editors joined the staff. The general format of the new magazine was quite similar to *The Masses*.

Miss Eastman was much impressed, as her reports in *The Liberator* indicate, with the success of Bela Kun in Hungary. In an address before the Central Council of the Soviet Republic in Hungary, she brought greetings from the American workingman and said that the "victory of the Russian proletariat which has come over to Hungary will spread to all the other countries of the world and likewise will lead to the liberation of the American proletariat."[8] Although she enthusiastically supported the revolution, her enthusiasm for war, even the ideological variety, was tempered when she witnessed its ravages. "Now I know there can be no such thing as a democratic army," she said in a report on conditions in Hungary. "People don't want to die, and except for a few glorious fanatics they are not going to vote themselves into the front line trenches."[9] The harshness of the war and the peace that followed convinced Miss Eastman that the price of victory was terribly high. But she still thought the cost of socialism worthwhile.

Miss Eastman's enthusiasm for the Kun regime as well as the communist regime in Russia alienated her from many liberal friends who had supported her in the feminist and pacifist movements. Before 1918 she had worked amicably with such liberals as Oswald Garrison Villard, Amos Pinchot, and Lillian Wald. But her energetic writings and speeches on the new Russia and the new Hungary cooled many of these friendships. When Miss Eastman devoted herself to political as opposed to cultural reform, liberals viewed her with suspicion.

In her reports on the American Socialist party for *The Liberator*, Miss Eastman continued the line of criticism that had characterized all of her brother Max's articles on the subject in *The Masses*. She criticized the Socialist party convention and platform in 1920 as being a patchwork of people and aims—something for everyone. "Their preamble," she commented, "could be taken over verbatim by Hiram Johnson if he should bolt the republican convention next week." Eugene Debs was their candidate, she wrote, because he was safely in jail "where he will lend them the glory of his name without the embarrassment of his clear thinking revolutionary leadership."[10] Her impatience with the party was clear in every line of her report.

In 1921 personal considerations as well as a growing interest in writing alone, removed from the burden of editing a magazine, led Crystal Eastman to withdraw from active management of *The Liberator*. Since the magazine's inception she had been managing editor as well as reporter. According to Max Eastman, his sister resigned because:

> I was beginning to realize that it had been, from Crystal's viewpoint, a mistake for her to join me in running *The Liberator*. Though our names stood equal on the masthead, and though her work and judgment were as important as mine, her position in the public mind was inevitably secondary. Crystal had her own eminence, and her own pride in it, but she was not primarily a writer—and on such a magazine all the wages of praise and appreciation went to the artists and writers.[11]

Crystal Eastman moved to England the following year with her husband Walter Fuller and her son. Max Eastman went to Russia where his admiration for Lenin was reinforced. *The Liberator* continued under the guidance of Claude McKay, Robert Minor, Joseph Freeman, and Mike Gold. It became, in 1922, the avowed voice of the Communist party and lost the wild spirit and independence it had displayed in its earlier days. Crystal Eastman continued to write about the dilemma of the modern woman in Labourite England. She did not find her utopia there, but she did discover a great many militant women.

Crystal Eastman's writing while in England provides an interesting view of one final form of feminism—perhaps a degeneration of the feminist position. She proposed to the London Sunday *Telegram* a weekly advice column called "Pandora's Box or What Is Your Trouble?"

In a sample piece she wrote for the editor, she defined the modern woman as being

> not altogether satisfied with love, marriage and a purely domestic career. She wants money of her own, she wants work of her own, she wants some means of self-expression, perhaps, some way of satisfying her personal ambitions. But she wants husband, home and children, too. How to reconcile these two desires in real life, that is the question.

There were innumerable Englishwomen, she told the editor, who would be eager to write about their problems and ask for help. She would answer their questions. For example, she provided this fictitious case study: How should the wife of a businessman spend her leisure time? Her children were raised and her youthful interest in music had gone undeveloped. In this mock column, Miss Eastman advised the lady to resume piano lessons.[12]

The column sounded very much like today's Ann Landers. Was Crystal Eastman prophetic? Did she come to believe, as current writers seem to, that the only meaningful way to deal with woman's problem was the individual approach? Had she abandoned all hope of a cultural revolution? Her modest proposal certainly suggests it. The possibility of legislative reform must have seemed inadequate to her. She had seen inheritance laws liberalized without any subsequent reappraisal of woman's pattern of living. She had seen many young women go to college in the 1920's without a significant change in styles of life. Even in those countries that had experienced a socio-political revolution, such as socialist England, the roles of women remained the same. Woman as wife and mother remained the universal pattern in Western society. A popular newspaper column that would reach many frustrated women may have seemed a workable alternative. But the *Telegram* rejected "Pandora's Box," and Crystal Eastman never was able to test her idea. She returned to the United States in 1927, dissatisfied with the progress of her literary career in England. Her husband had died suddenly of a cerebral hemorrhage before sailing, and Miss Eastman became ill with bronchial pneumonia soon after her return. She tried to work and began organizing the tenth anniversary celebration of Oswald Garrison Villard's *Nation*. But sickness overcame her; she died in August 1928 at the age of forty-seven.[13]

Thus none of the Village feminists continued the feminist debate into the 1920's. Except for Henrietta Rodman, they all left the Village and lived elsewhere. Not only did they fail to find an equally congenial environment for their feminism, but they had lost the spirit that had motivated them. They were older, tired of fighting, and discouraged by their failures. The war, probably more than anything else, was their downfall. They gave all of their attentions to its speedy conclusion and to educating women to the importance of preserving peace once they gained the vote. As it turned out, women did not seem to vote differently from men.[14] The feminist-pacifist argument that women would make the world safe for democracy and freedom was not borne out. Neither women nor men *really* believed that woman's role had to be changed.

For all of these reasons, the cultural debate over women's rights and opportunities did not continue into the twenties. The minority of women who carried the feminist banner during the 1910's (while the majority fought for suffrage) were no longer able or willing to carry on. After 1920, young and frivolous women in Greenwich Village accepted, ironically, only the romantic interpretation of feminism: the young woman's search for love and happiness. Experiment and experience became the sum total of the feminist view of the twenties—a rather incomplete analysis of the feminist ideology, to be sure, but the only one that young women were willing to accept. More serious-minded women joined the League of Women Voters and the Women's International League for Peace and Freedom, and contented themselves with lectures, study groups, and resolutions. They accepted the male view of their limitations.

The new Villagers did not need or want a cultural revolution to accomplish their aims; the bohemian Village offered them their place, and that was their sole interest. A hedonistic calm settled over Greenwich Village; pleasure was pursued more intensely than it had ever been in the pre-war Village. Villagers regarded Henrietta Rodman as an old eccentric and blithely ignored her. Society ladies shuddered at reminiscences of feminist behavior, and very quickly the Greenwich Village of 1910–1920 became part of the forgotten past.

❧

After a period of reflection, many Village feminists recorded their impressions of the prewar decade: Hutchins Hapgood's *A Victorian in the Modern World* (1939), Floyd Dell's *Homecoming* (1933) and *Intellectual Vagabondage: An Apology for the Intelligentsia* (1926), Max Eastman's *Enjoyment of Living* (1948), Susan Glaspell's *The Road to the Temple* (1927), Neith Boyce's unpublished autobiography, and Crystal Eastman's unpublished autobiographical sketch, "Modern Adventures in Maternity." All of these memoirs were similar in interesting ways. The men all spoke about the new women they had known and loved; the women all spoke about the problems of satisfying their maternal needs at the same time they pursued their intellectual quests.

Looking back, the male feminists saw the Greenwich Village phase of their lives as a time of experiment and youthful search. As Floyd Dell explained it:

> I don't think any of us quite knew what we believed about love and "freedom." We were in love with life, and willing to believe almost any modern theory which gave us a chance to live our lives more fully. We were incredibly well meaning.[15]

Romance, and the youthful search for identity, preoccupied Dell and his friends. Max Eastman portrayed his

early years in the Village as years of indoctrination into
the realities of life. Ida Rauh gave him his first introduction to Marx; Crystal Eastman initiated him into the life
of social action. "She pulled me downtown," he said, referring to his sister's influence.[16] Both Dell and Eastman
emerge, from their own remembrances, as naive searchers
who found the strong-willed women in their lives to be
both their delight and their guides.

Hutchins Hapgood described how he and his wife
Neith Boyce (who were no longer mere youths in 1910
but the parents of four children) felt about the restlessness of the young people of the Village as well as their own
gropings:

> Neith and I, like many another couple who on the
> whole were good fathers and mothers, were con-
> scious of the latent feminism urging men to give up
> the ascendancy which women thought they had,
> and women to demand from men that which they
> didn't really want, namely so-called freedom from
> the ideal of monogamy.

Hapgood revealed his adherence to the traditional male
view of feminism: women were trying to infringe upon
man's world. The universe was composed of ascendant
and descendant creatures; when women became assertive,
they threatened man's superior position. But Hapgood
demonstrated a more "typically" Village view when he
added that, during that period,

> there was still healthy vigor and moral idealism
> underlying the effort. So that the total result was

a working-out of the situation into a more conscious companionship, greater self-knowledge, and
a broader understanding of the relations between
the sexes.[17]

The goal was self-discovery which, in turn, would lead to
a mature relationship between men and women. Hapgood was not wholly sympathetic to the strivings of the
radical feminists. He still believed that woman's place
was in the home; though he enjoyed the companionship
of many feminists and admired his wife's writings, he still
wanted Neith to be at home with the children.

Like Hapgood, most male feminists found the restless young women in the Village exciting comrades; they
also saw them as symbols of the new age. Floyd Dell probably said it best:

The difference between the masculine and feminine
idealists of this period is now apparent. We were
content with what was happening to woman because what we wanted was something for ourselves
—a Glorious Playfellow. . . . But they wanted something different—something for themselves.[18]

In retrospect, Dell realized that to women, feminism had
serious implications. Max Eastman thought the feminists
were the only ones who really lived. He found the young
women vital, interesting, and interested in life. When his
wife Ida Rauh was expecting a child, Eastman complained
that she became apathetic. He wanted a playmate and a
companion, not a wife and mother.[19]

All of the male feminists agreed that woman's

emergence into the world of business, politics, and social action was one of the unique features of Village life; but not all of the male feminists understood what it meant or what the ultimate goals of the women feminists were. "We thought," Floyd Dell observed, "they would be content with the joy of struggle. But they needed the joy of achievement."[20] The men discovered, upon reflection, that they had miscalculated the aims of the emancipated woman. She was not content merely with the search; she wanted to see the fruits of her efforts. This disparity between the aims of the male and female feminists is crucial. Henrietta Rodman could not see the feminist movement as a pleasurable pastime or as a humorous game; when Floyd Dell made fun of the suffrage movement in his play *What Eight Million Women Want*, Miss Rodman was outraged; her reaction bewildered Dell at the time. Why get so excited about a glorious fight? The joy, according to Dell and his male colleagues, was in the process.

This romantic view of life's search was not sufficient for women feminists. Crystal Eastman wanted to see laws rewritten, attitudes changed, and values re-examined. All of the women feminists were also profoundly concerned with working out, in their personal lives, some reconciliation between their own needs and wishes and the possibilities of success. While Floyd Dell thought that all emancipated women wanted free love and would find it emotionally satisfying, Crystal Eastman wondered, at age twenty-six, "if I would get married in time to have children."[21] And Susan Glaspell, who never had any children of her own because of a heart lesion, woefully said: "Women say to one, 'you have your work. Your books are your children, aren't they?' And you look at the diapers airing by the fire, and wonder if they really think you are like that. . . ."²²

Like all women, the feminists had maternal needs. They too wanted to be wives and mothers, *but* they wanted other roles as well. They objected to the parameters of their traditional roles. The male feminist, on the other hand, saw the women in the Village as exceptional —as different from other women. They were carefree, intellectually exciting people who had abandoned the traditional life of home and family. The male feminists, it seems, made the same mistake that the public at large made: they thought women feminists were, in fact, *not* like other women. So they could not take them seriously —just as the larger society did not take them seriously.

Floyd Dell said that the women Villagers looked upon motherhood "as one of the most interesting of [life's] adventures."²³ But not necessarily the greatest, or the only, one. The women, however, took motherhood more seriously. Crystal Eastman wrote that she had always considered motherhood as the central experience in a woman's life. She related how, as a child, she had announced to her family that she wanted "to be the head of an orphan asylum so as to be sure to have enough children." When she was twenty-six and still unmarried, she decided upon a solution to her dilemma: "If she did not marry before the age of twenty-nine, she would go to

Italy, have a baby, and return with an 'adopted child.' "
As it turned out, she married seventeen days before her
twenty-ninth birthday.[24]

While the women feminists sought to fulfill their
maternal desires as well as their social and intellectual
needs, the men were engaged in their own personal search.
Floyd Dell, Hutchins Hapgood, and George Cram Cook
chronicled their disappointments in love and their efforts
to work out a formula for man-woman happiness. Cook,
whose writings were recorded in Susan Glaspell's volume
of reminiscences, wrote extensively on the ideal love relationship. He resisted possessing the woman he loved because he thought she would lose her individuality. "He
did not want to be her master," Miss Glaspell related.
"Her love as a free and equal soul was what he craved."[25]
Miss Glaspell explained that her husband saw the union
with a woman as one source of emotional and intellectual
fulfillment. "The Christian spirit is like an unmated
woman," he wrote; "the pagan spirit an unmated man.
Creative fruitfulness in mind and body lies in their rightful union."[26] In another passage Cook, whose love of love
seemed endless, proclaimed, "If a woman loved me
forever, it would be forever her gift and not my
right."[27]

Despite differences of emphasis, men and women
feminists shared a process of self-discovery; both were
interested in finding the limits of their capabilities; both
had an urge to experiment with life and explain the world
around them. The women's desire to be something more
than traditional women gave them the courage to fight for

the causes in which they believed. It was Crystal Eastman's dogged will that kept her fighting for peace when
many others had given up; it was Henrietta Rodman's
stubbornness that made her try one feminist crusade
after another.

The men's desires were not as difficult to satisfy: to
enjoy life and experience it fully. This usually meant sexual satisfaction and diversion; according to the stories of
Floyd Dell's love affairs in the Village, he seemed to work
hard at it. Greenwich Village society, of course, did not
frown upon this masculine interpretation of self-discovery.
While Henrietta Rodman was also reputed to have had
many love affairs, personal happiness did not seem to be
enough for her. Social change required serious campaign-
ing. Private satisfactions, though obviously important, did
not define her reason for being. The women feminists
wanted to see changes that reached beyond the boundaries
of their lives as well as those of the Village.

In one sense, man-woman roles were reversed in
Greenwich Village. It was the women who were the social
activists and the men who were the literary propagandists.
The women were more aggressive. Max Eastman and
Floyd Dell wrote indignantly about the ills of society, but
Crystal Eastman and Henrietta Rodman went into the
streets to do something about it. Max Eastman protested
the treatment his wife Ida Rauh received when she was
arrested for distributing birth-control pamphlets, but it
was Mrs. Eastman and not her husband who had performed the act. Women Villagers came out of the home
with a vengeance.

Because of the traditional definitions of male and female roles in our culture, whenever the woman leaves the home for activities other than approved "womanly" chores, she is criticized for intruding into the man's world. The term "aggressive," when applied to the feminist's militancy in social reforms, is a male term that reflects male cultural standards. This is precisely what Charlotte Perkins Gilman and her followers complained about: in an androcentric culture, the cards are stacked against feminist changes. Whenever women do anything that is normally done by men, they are accused of being manly; this criticism is supposed to silence them and halt their deviations. Another part of the androcentric culture is, after all, that no real woman would want to be like a man or do what a man does. This is the vicious circle that the feminists tried to break.

It is a vicious circle which the male feminists could not fully appreciate—first because of their romantic natures, and second because they were not women. Although Crystal Eastman and Henrietta Rodman displayed a great steadiness of purpose, they too must have wondered at times if their male critics' remarks were accurate: Did they really wish to be men in some psychological sense? Was their crusading a sign of inner weakness? Were they being good mothers (especially in Crystal Eastman's case, since she had a small son to care for while she agitated for peace)? Could they, or all women for that matter, be effective in other roles? Intellectually, the women always answered the question affirmatively; but in their heart of hearts, the answer might differ depending upon the circumstances.

❦

The Village feminists were an "intellectual community." By various standards they qualified as a self-conscious group of intellectuals who valued ideas and tried to make abstract principles the basis for their actions. They were genuinely excited by the latest theories of Freud, by the economic analyses of Marx and Lenin, and by the utopianism of the anarchists. Crystal Eastman, during the winter of 1917–1918, established a communal dwelling with her family, her brother Max, and many of their friends. They all shared a house, ate together, and tried optimistically to live cooperatively. The communal experiment did not last very long; each member's personal life drew him away from the common dwelling. But the attempt demonstrated their sincere commitment to utopian ideals.

The pre-war Village contained a mixture of poets and politicians. Writers fraternized with socialist activists and Wobblies patronized Mabel Dodge Luhan's Fifth Avenue salon. Theoreticians as well as practitioners were highly regarded. Both Charlotte Perkins Gilman and Henrietta Rodman were respected for their separate contributions to feminist reform. Both Margaret Sanger and Emma Goldman received high marks for their particular brand of activism. Academicians from Columbia mingled with the Villagers, and journalists such as Lincoln Steffens and Walter Lippmann were indoctrinated into avant-garde thinking through their Village contacts. During the war, when pacifism became an unpopular ideology, die-hard pacifists could always find sympathizers in the Village. Because Greenwich Village was a community, each member always felt comfortable there and able to communicate with soulmates.

The Villager's importance in his own community made his attitude toward the public at large ambivalent. On the one hand, the Village intellectual wanted to see major changes throughout society; on the other, he was content with the minor influence he had in his own community and needed no other. Floyd Dell was delighted with the feminists he knew and did not care to proselytize all womankind. Max Eastman, in contrast, seemed to be attracted by greater power. He enjoyed the fact that he had met with President Wilson and hoped that his views had influenced the President. Eastman might consider himself an outsider taking potshots at the Establishment, but he would probably have seized an opportunity to participate in changing the established order. Crystal Eastman's propaganda work and Henrietta Rodman's feminist program both assumed that their feminist ideology could be translated into general social practices, and that they could suggest specific reforms. To them the Village became a model that could be reproduced in society as a whole. Henrietta Rodman's apartment house for professional women and Crystal Eastman's plan for government aid to working-class mothers were not designed only for Villagers; all women could, and should, benefit from them.

While male feminists Floyd Dell and Max Eastman hoped that the socialist scheme could be implemented throughout society, they did not believe free love had the same chance. Dell considered the love arrangements of the Village unique to a bohemian community. Crystal Eastman looked at the uninhibited love relationships in the Village and saw the basis for a more natural marriage arrangement, one in which both parties benefited, and one which could be both entered and ended easily. To her the Village experiment had larger social implications. She believed that the family, that institution which most significantly affected women, required changing as much as the capitalistic order. A change in the economic sphere without a corresponding change in the family structure would not benefit women. Thus male and female feminists differed in this important respect: the men, like Floyd Dell, saw love in Greenwich Village as a gay, romantic quest enjoyed by the intellectual elite; the women, like Crystal Eastman, saw it as the microcosm of the future society for all people.

❦

The Village feminists have a number of unique intellectual credits. Perhaps most important, they perceived the "cultural lag" in society that was a result of industrialism. Although they did not coin the term, they applied Lester Ward's principle of an evolutionary social system and recognized that while the mechanical-technical parts of American culture were undergoing tremendous change, the social structure and the value system were not keeping pace. The class system and antiquated customs regarding women persisted while mass production was creating a new kind of economic life. The value changes which the feminists so strenuously fought for were essential, they contended, in making life in the twentieth century worthwhile. The individual's potential ought to be applied to readjusting man's ideas and practices to the new world. And it was the role of the intellectual to point the way for the rest of society to follow.

That the Village intellectuals were unable to effect the reforms they sought suggests an interesting commentary on social change in American culture. In so-called primitive culture, the introduction of a steel knife—a modest example of the new industrialism—brought real turbulence to social relations. In the case of one particular tribe, for example, the knife became the prized possession of the man in the family and was invested with all kinds of ritual significance. When the Westerner arrived on the scene and indiscriminately gave knives to every woman and child around, he unknowingly upset the whole hierarchial arrangement of the culture and destroyed the basis of human relationships. Nothing of the sort happened in this country when industrialism was introduced. Drastic changes in the economic sphere of life have not caused a value revolution. Social classes have shifted and sexual practices have changed, but values have not. Americans still think that the woman's place is in the home with her automatic dishwasher. Traditional man-woman roles have not been seriously changed or challenged.

This may be due to the American's flexibility and ingenious talent for interpreting industrial changes *within* accepted value and role patterns. It may also be due to the overarching view that if America succeeded materially because of men, then men should continue to determine the major values of the society. Or, put another way, if Americans became so rich and powerful with the family and the traditional structure operating, then why change?

Only the feminists among their contemporaries even questioned traditional man-woman roles. Unlike the suffragists, male and female, who believed that the vote was the key to emancipation, the woman feminists wanted a total revamping of society. Their vision, a blend of feminism and socialist philosophy, was, they claimed, an accurate, vital explanation of a future industrial, urban culture. They recognized the problems associated with such a culture and proposed ways of solving them. They perceived the advantages of industrialism but wanted them to benefit women, too—and not only in terms of time-saving devices in the home. Birth-control knowledge alone provides the basis for women to redefine their life roles, but not without an accompanying change in attitudes.

The Village feminists predicted the dissatisfied, troubled housewife of the 1960's, though most did not live to see the rebirth of feminism. They correctly foresaw that modern culture, without a corresponding change of values, would produce unhappy women, much like those whom Susan Glaspell created in her fiction. The feminists' analysis led them to different solutions to the problem: Henrietta Rodman thought professional training would free the frustrated woman; with specialized education, woman could be released from the home and lead a productive life in a world usually limited to men. Crystal Eastman argued for a socialist state whose government would support needy mothers; where education would be the same for boys and girls; and where state nurseries would care for the children of mothers who chose to work.

Susan Glaspell and Neith Boyce wanted to see an American culture that would tolerate the searching and striving young woman and not frown upon her sexual indiscretions. Miss Glaspell and Miss Boyce both thought the young girl needed a period of initiation into life. She ought to experience some of the joys and sorrows of living, then settle down to the business of being a wife and mother. This interpretation of the proper relationship between the individual and society has often been advanced for young men, but never before had it been suggested as appropriate behavior for a young girl. Presumably the inquisitive young woman would be willing to conform to the dictates of society after she had tasted some of the fruits of life. This proposal did not threaten the existing order; it only required a patient and tolerant society. Feminists more radical than Susan Glaspell or Neith Boyce, on the other hand, were not satisfied with this lesser goal.

The New Woman?

The new psychology had taught Crystal Eastman and Henrietta Rodman that women had sexual urges that needed expression; they also learned, from the science of anthropology, that each culture defined its human roles. From all of this they concluded that women could not become whole human beings until they broke loose from society's bounds—both its sexual and social restraints. Further, they realized that women were treated as dependents and conformed to this image themselves; they did not consider themselves qualified to run for political office, compete in the business world, or hold down a responsible job. The external, cultural definition of women as inferior also became their own internal view. Women were, after all, the products of their culture. The woman's identity, then, needed revamping. Before they could develop a new sense of security, women had to give up their secure but dependent identity and grope for a new, more human sense of themselves. The period of transition would not be easy. Crystal Eastman knew, from personal experience, how hard it was to be a good mother, wife, and social reformer. She knew that social institutions were not set up for feminist success. But she also knew that a radical change had to occur within women's minds as well as within the structures of society. Women had to free themselves in spite of society. And society, it was hoped, would change to accommodate the new woman. But, as Henrietta Rodman frequently said, women had to give up their child status and become adult before society would take notice of the changed woman.

As another example of their uniqueness, Village

feminists were among the first propagandists and agitators to use the modern media of communication. For the first time in American history, women reformers could reach a substantial audience through newspapers, movies, and telegrams. Crystal Eastman used all of these methods as well as such traditional ones as the public meeting and the protest demonstration. Through the mass media the country came to know the Village feminists as very different from nineteenth-century suffragists and reformers. All of the Village feminists were married women, most were mothers, and none was mannish according to stereotyped images. The masculine spinster picture of the woman reformer—a tactic, incidentally, that did a lot to keep women in their place—did not wash. These feminists came largely from the professional class: Crystal Eastman was an attorney, as was Ida Rauh; Henrietta Rodman was a teacher; and Neith Boyce and Susan Glaspell were newspaper reporters and professional writers. They were not, like Jane Addams, well-meaning women who were looking for an outlet for their energies.

Their fight was a principled one, without the kind of emotional hoopla that had accompanied the suffrage movement. Although Crystal Eastman employed some histrionics in her peace campaign, her feminist writings and activities were rationally conceived and executed with dignity. Henrietta Rodman's Feminist Alliance advocated a feminist apartment house with the utmost seriousness and no dramatic flourish. The women worked diligently for feminism at the same time they fought for socialism,

birth control, and peace. All of these campaigns contributed, from their point of view, to the achievement of
their utopia.

The Village feminists were similar to earlier reformers, however, in terms of background. Crystal Eastman's ancestors came to America in the early seventeenth
century; twenty-three editors of *Four Lights* qualified for
membership in the Daughters of the American Revolution. The Village feminists were, in other words, products
of old American families. They nonetheless displayed the
same fiery impatience that characterized working women
reformers such as Emma Goldman and Elizabeth Gurley
Flynn. The Village feminists may have enjoyed greater
freedom than most American women, but they were still
unsatisfied with traditional attitudes toward women. Together, the dignified, educated feminist and the lower-
class woman agitator during the decade 1910–1920
formed a new force of women reformers—believers in
direct action, articulate social philosophers, impatient
implementers of their beliefs.

In terms of age the Village feminists fell between
the suffragist leadership and the radical-immigrant reformers. In 1910 all were around thirty years old. No
longer blushing and uninitiated, they were not yet the
veterans that Carrie Chapman Catt and Anna Howard
Shaw were either. They were young enough to work with
the Elizabeth Gurley Flynns and old enough to be taken
seriously by Mrs. Catt. They had already been to college,
had worked for a while in New York City, and knew

something about living and working in the city. They had the enthusiasm of youth combined with the purpose and conviction that come from personal experience.

Here, then, was the uniqueness of the Village feminists: they perceived many of the difficulties of life for women in an urban, industrial culture; they understood the idea of cultural lag without ever having heard the term; and they coupled their feminist beliefs with their socialist philosophy for a comprehensive socio-economic and cultural alternative to the contemporary situation. As a group they exhibited the traits of an intellectual class, destroyed the old-fashioned stereotype of the spinster reformer, and combined an old American background with professional training to offer a new image of the woman reformer. They were propagandists and publicists as well as plain old agitators. They systematically used communications media to inform the public of their beliefs. They continued to discuss feminism while most women only discussed the vote. After the war, when the nation settled down to forget their troubles, the feminists renewed their discussion of woman's needs in the twentieth century.

❦

Their failures, unfortunately, were greater than their successes. As they became more unique, so they became more unsuccessful. That is to say, their uniqueness took them further and further away from majority interests and concerns. As they devised bold new feminist schemes, they lost touch with most women and men around them. That they had a supportive group in the Village contributed to this separation. The Village feminists encouraged novel and radical solutions to problems; they strenuously supported every adventure. Thus they could feed upon the enthusiasm of their friends rather than seek new links with the outside world. The radical-feminist involvement in the pacifist movement during the war also alienated them from most Americans.

The feminists left no viable organization to carry on their work. The Feminist Alliance, a by-product of Henrietta Rodman's imagination, participated only in causes that appealed to Miss Rodman. When her attention was diverted by other crusades, the feminist program fell by the wayside. The National American Woman's Suffrage Association was not interested in beginning a new program in 1920. One-tenth of its membership became the League of Women Voters and devoted itself to nonpartisan civic betterment. The League did not encourage its experienced leaders to run for political office now that they had the vote; neither did it campaign for politicians who advocated women's rights. Although it developed an impressive legislative program in the twenties, the League did not capitalize upon the woman's vote. Its leadership remained moderate and unwilling to fuss about anything. Even the radical suffragist Alice Paul, who formed the National Woman's party, was indifferent to a feminist program. She concentrated on the equal rights amendment and argued that all other proposals (such as the ones Crystal Eastman suggested at the NWP's 1920 convention) were superfluous. The Woman's Peace party, which, according to Miss Eastman, was another natural vehicle for feminist action, became part of the Women's International League for Peace and Freedom, and remained strictly a pacifist organization. Thus none of the existing women's organizations carried on the feminist campaign. Most women's organizations in the twenties refused to discuss abortion, birth control, or liberalized divorce laws. Although the woman's lobby in Washington during the twenties (representing the most prestigious women's organizations) supported federal aid to education and standardized educational facilities, they did not discuss the need to provide equal educational opportunity for boys and girls. The feminist voice was silent during the twenties.

Another crucial failing of the feminists was their attempt to do too many things at once—with too little ammunition. While their comprehensive view and their sense of the interrelatedness of reform activities was one of their strengths, it also prevented them from working personally in all of the separate reform groups with which they agreed. Nor were they able to bring them together into a single meaningful movement. The feminists saw the connection between the working class, the middle-class leadership, and the good-willed aristocrats, but they were unable to build a political coalition or an economic bloc which could wield power. Crystal Eastman suggested "women's power" as a tool to be used after women gained the vote; but she was never able to put together enough support for the idea to make it work. The feminists could not inspire their followers sufficiently to commit them to the long haul. In typical reform fashion, too many women breathed a sigh of relief and returned to their private lives when the vote was won, when the war ended, and when the New York Board of Education granted maternity leaves. There were not many Crystal Eastmans or Henrietta Rodmans who were willing to devote their whole lives to feminism.

Most important, perhaps, the feminists discovered that American society would allow itself to be reformed only when it did not consider itself seriously threatened. Teacher-mothers in the classroom posed no danger to the existing order. As long as there was no state control of birth-control information or free medical advice, the demands of the birth-control advocates were not troublesome. But pacifism and feminism did attack the fundamental structure of society. Because pacifism imperiled the safety of the country, it was a dangerous ideology. Feminism revolutionized traditional roles and was therefore un-American. Feminism might be laughed off; pacifists had to be stopped.

Thus, while feminists failed partly because of their inability to marshall support for their beliefs, it was more decisive that the substance of their program was too radically removed from reality.

❦

The 1960's produced a new feminism. After a lull of more than forty years, serious debate once more erupted over the restraints society placed upon women. Many

young women joined women's liberation groups in protest. They worked at de-acculturating themselves, at re-
moving from their consciousness their culturally defined
roles. They tried to communicate their liberated message
to their "sisters," as they called all women. In language
franker and bolder than the Village feminists used, they
showed anger, hostility, resentment, and frustration. It is
not easy to account for this reinvigoration, but part of the
answer may rest with the mistaken popular view of
emancipation held in the 1920's.

The flapper thought she was free. Indeed, society
at large believed that with women voting, working in
greater numbers, and owning property, they would be
equal to men. The fact of psychological dependence, of
women seeing themselves as subservient to men, as men
saw them, received little attention. Professional women
seemed to agree with this popular analysis: they devoted
themselves to their careers and ignored serious reform
work. Those who continued with Alice Paul's National
Woman's party fought for an equal rights amendment
but could not keep the feminist cause before the public.
Women who were interested in protective legislation for
working women also had an uphill struggle throughout
the twenties. That organization women did not continue
the discussion of women's roles is a telling cultural fact.

The civil rights and New Left movements of the
1960's engaged a generation of college students in an
unprecedented way. In the course of their crusading,
many radical young women became aware of a disturbing

fact: radical men were male chauvinists. They shared the culture's traditional role definition of women. They assigned women secretarial and clerical chores while they did the revolutionary planning. Max Eastman and Floyd Dell had tried to practice egalitarianism, but Stokely Carmichael was quoted as saying that the place for young women was under young men. So some of the radical women decided to free themselves. Just as women abolitionists a hundred years earlier had separated from the black movement and formed the suffrage movement, so radical young women of the sixties became women's liberationists. The leadership of this movement, which is still amorphous and embraces many different groups and shades of opinion, came from the same middle class that had produced suffrage and feminist leaders earlier in the century.

Feminist writers of the sixties found in women's liberation both comfort and support in numbers. The mass media, always hungry for novelty, gobbled up the subject, usually vulgarizing and distorting its message. All the same, the feminism of the sixties may enjoy a longer life than the movement in the 1910's. More young women have been exposed to feminism's message; the pill has made birth control a real possibility; and the hippie's communal style of living has affected middle-class youth in significant ways. Conventional marriage with a house in the suburbs has lost its appeal for large numbers of young people. Feminism's message, on the other hand, fits right in with the new humanism and pacifism that characterize the philosophy of the under-thirty generation. While third-grade girls demand courses in woodworking, educational publishers are revamping their textbooks to show girls in traditionally male-designated roles. Specifics such as these, advocated by Village feminists more than fifty years ago, are being implemented for the first time in American history. If children are raised equally and girls are taught to believe that the full range of human roles is available to them, feminism may succeed.

Crystal Eastman could not interest the under-thirty generation in feminism in 1920, but Betty Friedan, Kate Millett, and Shulamith Firestone have found an audience. These women, sharing much in common with the Village feminists, have the advantage of facing a bolder, more socially conscious generation than the one that was coming of age in 1920. Still, feminism's fundamental problem—to reconcile an essentially radical solution with liberal-moderate means—has not been resolved. Those feminists who ally themselves with the Third World movement and see feminism as part of a larger world revolution do not have much chance for success. Those feminists who use typical reform methods of propaganda and direct action within the system must content themselves with, at best, piecemeal changes. This vicious circle has not been broken.

The radical feminists of the sixties and seventies may find American society unwilling to adopt their most sweeping proposals, such as the restructuring of the family; but the very radicalness of such suggestions may make more moderate feminist demands appear reasonable. Had Crystal Eastman and Henrietta Rodman lived into the sixties and seventies, they may have seen educational and professional equality for women, government assistance for mothers, and state-run day-care nurseries. They *may* have. The vision is still blurred, but surely the dream of the Greenwich Village feminists has been reborn in the hearts and minds of current women's liberationists. Better luck to them.

Notes

CHAPTER 1. A STAGE FOR REBELLION

1. Floyd Dell, *Homecoming* (New York: Farrar and Rinehart, 1933), p. 246.
2. Aileen S. Kraditor, *The Ideas of the Woman's Suffrage Movement, 1890–1920* (New York: Columbia University Press, 1965), p. 11.
3. *Ibid.*, p. xi.
4. Interview with Mrs. Ida Rauh Eastman, August 30, 1966.
5. Floyd Dell, *Intellectual Vagabondage* (New York: George H. Doran, 1926), p. 161.
6. Max Eastman, *Enjoyment of Living* (New York: Harcourt, Brace, 1948), p. 26.
7. *Ibid.*, p. 266.
8. *Ibid.*, p. 267.
9. *Ibid.*, p. 341.
10. *Ibid.*, p. 357.
11. Floyd Dell, *Love in Greenwich Village* (New York: George H. Doran, 1926), p. 18.
12. Interview with Mrs. Ida Rauh Eastman, August 30, 1966.
13. Eastman, *Enjoyment of Living*, p. 267.
14. Interview with Mrs. Eastman.
15. Quoted in Eastman, *Enjoyment of Living*, pp. 379–380.
16. Neith Boyce, "Unpublished Autobiography," p. 153, in Neith Boyce and Hutchins Hapgood Collection, Beinecke Rare Book and Manuscript Library, Yale University. Cited hereafter as Hapgood Collection.
17. *Ibid.*, p. 135.
18. Mabel Dodge Luhan, *Movers and Shakers*, vol. 3 of *Intimate Memories* (New York: Harcourt, Brace, 1936), p. 48.

(153)

19. *Ibid.*, p. 187.

20. Susan Glaspell, *The Road to the Temple* (New York: Frederick A. Stokes, 1927), p. 247.

CHAPTER 2. AN IDEOLOGY DEVELOPS

1. Winnifred Harper, "The Younger Suffragists," *Harper's Weekly*, LVIII (September 27, 1913), 7–8.

2. *Ibid.*, p. 7.

3. Carl Degler, "Charlotte Perkins Gilman on the Theory and Practice of Feminism," *American Quarterly*, VIII (Spring 1956), 22.

4. Mrs. Gilman's books include *Women and Economics* (Boston: Small, Maynard, 1898) and *The Man-Made World or Our Androcentric Culture* (New York: Charleton, 1911).

5. Charlotte Perkins Gilman, "Are Women Human Beings?," *Harper's Weekly*, LVI (May 25, 1912), 11.

6. Charlotte Perkins Gilman, "The Waste of Private Housekeeping," *Annals of the American Academy of Political and Social Science*, XLVIII (July 1913), 91.

7. *Ibid.*, p. 95.

8. Crystal Eastman, "Now Let Us Begin," *The Liberator*, II (December 1920), 23.

9. *New York Times*, January 24, 1915, Part V, p. 9.

10. Crystal Eastman, "Now Let Us Begin," p. 24.

11. *Ibid.*

12. Crystal Eastman, "Alice Paul's Convention," *The Liberator*, IV (April 1921), 10.

13. Charlotte Perkins Gilman, "Charlotte Perkins Gilman's Dynamic Social Philosophy," *Current Literature*, LI (July 1911), 9.

14. *New York Times*, January 24, 1915, p. 9.

15. Crystal Eastman, "Are Wives Partners or Dependents?" (unpublished manuscript, n.d.), p. 3, in possession of Max Eastman.

16. Susan Glaspell, "The Rules of the Institution," *Harper's Magazine*, CXXVIII (January 1914), 208.

17. Susan Glaspell, *Fidelity* (Boston: Small, Maynard, 1915), p. 208.

Notes

18. Floyd Dell, *Janet March* (New York: Alfred A. Knopf, 1923), p. 152.
19. *Ibid.*, p. 456.
20. Glaspell, *Fidelity*, p. 41.
21. Dell, *Janet March*, p. 153.
22. Neith Boyce, "The Return," *Harper's Weekly*, LX (January 9, 1915), 42.
23. Neith Boyce, "The Wife of a Genius," *Harper's Weekly*, LIX (December 12, 1914), 566–568.
24. Glaspell, *Fidelity*, p. 59.
25. Floyd Dell, "The Kitten and the Masterpiece," in *Love in Greenwich Village* (New York: George H. Doran, 1926), pp. 72–73.
26. Floyd Dell, "The Rise of Greenwich Village," in *ibid.*, p. 43.
27. Mary Heaton Vorse, *I've Come to Stay* (New York: Century, 1915), p. 75.
28. Floyd Dell, "The Ex-Villager's Confession," in *Love in Greenwich Village*, p. 250.
29. Vorse, *I've Come to Stay*, p. 110.
30. Neith Boyce, "Art and Woman" (unpublished manuscript, n.d.), p. 8, Hapgood Collection.
31. Neith Boyce to Mabel Dodge Luhan, undated, pp. 2–3, Hapgood Collection.
32. *Ibid.*, p. 1.
33. Reported in Eastman, *Enjoyment of Living*, pp. 379–80.
34. Susan Glaspell, *The Verge* (Boston: Small, Maynard, 1922).
35. Hutchins Hapgood, *A Victorian in the Modern World* (New York: Harcourt, Brace, 1939), p. 377.
36. Susan Glaspell, "Bernice," *Plays* (Boston: Small, Maynard, 1920).
37. Susan Glaspell, *A Jury of Her Peers* (London: Ernest Benn, 1927).

CHAPTER 3. PRACTICING THE THEORY

1. Andrew Sinclair, *The Emancipation of the American*

Notes

Woman (paperback ed.; New York: Harper and Row, 1965), pp. 293–296.

2. Inez Haynes Irwin, *The Story of the Woman's Party* (New York: Harcourt, Brace, 1921), pp. 51, 66.

3. Miss Eastman argued that feminism could only be a meaningful philosophy in a peaceful world; therefore her list of priorities demanded that she devote herself to the peace movement during wartime.

4. *New York Times*, April 5, 1914, Part IV, p. 4.

5. *Ibid.*, April 13, 1914, p. 6.

6. *Ibid.*, April 22, 1914, p. 12.

7. *Ibid.*, April 5, 1914, Part IV, p. 4.

8. *Ibid.*, January 24, 1915, Part V, p. 9.

9. *Ibid.*, April 25, 1915, Part V, p. 21.

10. Quoted in K. W. Baker, " 'Raising' Babies," *The Masses*, VIII (February 1916), 18.

11. *New York Times*, January 24, 1915, Part V, p. 9.

12. *Ibid.*, December 31, 1914, p. 1.

13. Max Eastman, "An Oz. of Prevention," *The Masses*, IV (August 1913), 1.

14. *New York Times*, reports throughout October and November 1914.

15. Floyd Dell, "Our Village School Board," *The Masses*, VI (March 1915), 11.

16. *New York Times*, November 13, 1914, p. 10.

17. *Ibid.*, October 11, 1914, Part II, p. 15.

18. *New York Tribune*, November 10, 1914, p. 8.

19. *Ibid.*, November 12, 1914, p. 8.

20. *New York Times*, November 15, 1914, Part II, p. 13.

21. *Ibid.*, December 16, 1914, p. 8.

22. *Ibid.*, December 24, 1914, p. 11.

23. *Ibid.*, January 23, 1915, p. 8; January 28, 1915, p. 1.

24. *Ibid.*, March 1, 1915, p. 4.

25. *Ibid.*, December 31, 1914, p. 1; January 12, 1915, p. 1.

26. *Ibid.*, June 24, 1915, p. 11.

27. Unsigned editorial, "Free Speech for Teachers," *New Republic*, III (June 26, 1915), 193.

Notes

28. Unsigned editorial, "Discipline of New York City Teachers," *School and Society*, IV (August 12, 1916), 259.

29. *New York Times*, December 27, 1914, Part II, p. 6.

30. Robert Latou Dickinson, a noted gynecologist, changed his mind twice during the 1920's about when, in a woman's menstrual cycle, conception occurred. See Chapter 7, "Birth Control and American Medicine," in David Kennedy's *Birth Control in America: The Career of Margaret Sanger* (New Haven: Yale University Press, 1970) for a discussion of this subject.

31. Margaret Sanger, *Woman and the New Race* (New York: Blue Ribbon Books, 1920), p. 1.

32. For more information on the life and career of Margaret Sanger, see Kennedy, *Birth Control in America*, and Emily Taft Douglas, *Margaret Sanger: Pioneer of the Future* (New York: Holt, Rinehart and Winston, 1970).

33. Max Eastman, "Revolutionary B-Control," *The Masses*, VI (July 1915), 22.

34. *Ibid.*, p. 21.

35. Max Eastman, "Is the Truth Obscene?," *The Masses*, VI (March 1915), 9.

36. Emma Goldman, "Testimony Before a Court on April 20, 1916," *The Masses*, VIII (June 1916), 27.

37. Henrietta Rodman to Mary Heaton Vorse, March 14, 1916, in Mary Heaton Vorse Manuscript Collection, Wayne State University Library.

38. Unsigned article, *The Masses*, VIII (July 1916), 27.

39. Interview with Mrs. Ida Rauh Eastman, August 30, 1966.

40. Jessie Ashley, "Successful Law-Breaking," *The Masses*, IX (January 1917), 16.

41. A. G. [Arturo Giovanitti?], "Careful District Attorney," *The Masses*, VII (August 1916), 23.

42. Ashley, "Successful Law-Breaking," p. 16.

43. *Ibid.*, p. 17.

44. Floyd Dell, *The Outline of Marriage* (American Birth Control League, n.d.), in the Floyd Dell Manuscript Collection (Newberry Library, Chicago, Illinois). Cited hereafter as the Dell Collection.

Notes

CHAPTER 4. FEMINIST ORGANIZATIONS, VILLAGE STYLE

1. Andrew Sinclair discusses this in his book *The Emancipation of the American Woman*, pp. 255–257.

2. Dell's philosophy is discussed later in this chapter.

3. Art Young, *On My Way* (New York: Liveright, 1928), pp. 268–269.

4. Max Eastman, *Enjoyment of Living*, p. 315.

5. *Ibid.*, p. 316.

6. Hapgood, *A Victorian in the Modern World*, p. 314.

7. Dell, *Homecoming*, p. 164.

8. Floyd Dell, "Feminism for Men," *Looking at Life* (New York: Alfred A. Knopf, 1924), pp. 17–23.

9. Floyd Dell, "Review of *The Sexual Crisis* by Grete Meisel-Hess," *The Masses*, IX (April 1917), 26.

10. Floyd Dell, "Confessions of a Feminist Man," undated extract from *The Masses*, Dell Collection.

11. Floyd Dell, "Mona Lisa and the Wheelbarrow," *Looking at Life*, pp. 1–10.

12. Floyd Dell, *Love in the Machine Age* (New York: Farrar and Rinehart, 1930).

13. Dell, *Intellectual Vagabondage*, p. 130.

14. Floyd Dell, "Literature and the Machine Age," *The Liberator*, VI (June 1924), 28.

15. Floyd Dell, *Women as World Builders: Studies in Modern Feminism* (Chicago: Forbes, 1913), p. 44.

16. Floyd Dell, "Literature and the Machine Age," *The Liberator*, VI (May 1924), 27.

17. Max Eastman, "Confessions of a Suffrage Orator," *The Masses*, VII (October-November 1915), 8.

18. *Ibid.*, p. 9.

19. Advertisement by Alice Carpenter, Zona Gale, Anna Strunsky Walling, Marie Jenney Howe, and Vira Boarman Whitehouse, *The Masses*, VIII (February 1916), 1.

20. Max Eastman, *The Masses*, IV (May 1913), 6–8; and the Art Young cartoon, pp. 9–10 of the same issue.

Notes

21. James Henle, "Nobody's Sister," *The Masses*, VI (January 1915), 10.

22. "A Strange Meeting," *The Masses*, IX (April 1917), 21, 24.

23. Charles W. Wood, "Thoughts on God and Annette Kellermann," *The Masses*, IX (March 1917), 32.

24. Floyd Dell, "The Nature of Women," *The Masses*, VIII (January 1916), 16.

25. For at least six months before American entry into the war in April 1917, these themes characterized *The Masses*. Crystal Eastman argued substantially the same position. Her views and activities during wartime are dealt with in the following chapter.

26. Dell, *Homecoming*, pp. 260–266.

27. *New York Times*, July 24, 1963, p. 25.

28. Hapgood, *A Victorian in the Modern World*, p. 393.

29. Lawrence Langner, *The Magic Curtain* (New York: E. P. Dutton, 1951), p. 67.

30. Dell, *Homecoming*, p. 265.

31. Arthur E. Waterman, "A Critical Study of Susan Glaspell's Works and Her Contributions to Modern American Drama" (unpublished Ph.D. dissertation, Department of English, University of Wisconsin, 1956), p. 99.

32. John Reed, "Minute Book of the Provincetown Players, Inc.," September 5, 1916, in the Provincetown Players Theater Collection (Research Library of the Performing Arts, New York Public Library at Lincoln Center).

33. Interview with Mrs. Ida Rauh Eastman, August 30, 1966.

34. Dell, *Homecoming*, p. 266.

35. Waterman, "A Critical Study of Susan Glaspell's Works . . .," p. 89.

36. George T. Tanselle, "Faun at the Barricades: The Life and Work of Floyd Dell" (unpublished Ph.D. dissertation, Department of English, Northwestern University, 1959), p. 188.

37. Dell, *Homecoming*, p. 262.

38. Floyd Dell, "King Arthur's Socks," *King Arthur's Socks and Other Village Plays* (New York: Alfred A. Knopf, 1922), p. 46.

39. *Ibid.*, p. 59.
40. Glaspell, "Woman's Honor," *Plays*, p. 156.
41. Glaspell, *A Jury of Her Peers*, p. 35.
42. Ludwig Lewisohn, *The Nation*, VIII (November 3, 1920), 509.
43. Mary Heaton Vorse, *Time and the Town: A Provincetown Chronicle* (New York: Dial Press, 1942), p. 124.
44. *Current Opinion*, LXV (July 1918), 28–29.
45. *Ibid.*, p. 28.
46. Interview with Mrs. Ida Rauh Eastman, August 30, 1966.
47. Lewisohn, *The Nation*, VIII (November 3, 1920), 509.
48. Dell, *Homecoming*, p. 266.
49. Neith Boyce, "Iowa to Delphi," p. 5, Hapgood Collection.

CHAPTER 5. THE CHALLENGE OF WAR

1. Sinclair, *The Emancipation of the American Woman*, p. 288.
2. Crystal Eastman Benedict, "To Make War Unthinkable" (letter), *New Republic*, III (July 24, 1915), 313.
3. Crystal Eastman, "A Program for Voting Women," March 1918, Woman's Peace Party Collection.
4. Woman's Peace Party, "Preamble to the Program," *The Survey*, XXXIII (January 23, 1915), 434.
5. Vorse, *A Footnote to Folly*, p. 79.
6. Mary Heaton Vorse, "The Sinistrees of France," *Century Magazine*, CXXII (January 1917), 450.
7. Mabel Dodge, "The Secret of War," *The Masses*, VI (November 1914), 9.
8. Joseph O'Brien, "Men and Guns," *Harper's Weekly*, LX (May 8, 1915), 441.
9. It is necessary to distinguish between the national Woman's Peace party, headed by Jane Addams, and the New York chapter of Crystal Eastman. The two groups split after 1917 and Jane Addams disavowed the actions of the more radical New York branch.
10. Boardman Robinson, *Four Lights*, I (September 8, 1917), 2–3.

Notes

11. Howard Brubaker, "Definitionaries to the Heathens," *Four Lights*, I (March 24, 1917), 3; Max Eastman, "Conscription," *Four Lights*, I (February 24, 1917), 3.

12. Mary Alden Hopkins, "Woman's Way in War," *Four Lights*, I (June 2, 1917), 4.

13. *Four Lights* Press Release, August 13, 1917, Woman's Peace Party Collection.

14. Freda Kirchway and Madeline Z. Doty, *Four Lights*, I (March 24, 1917), 4.

15. Anna Howard Shaw, "Votes for Women," *Four Lights*, I (February 24, 1917), 2.

16. Press Release, November 25, 1915, pp. 1–2, Woman's Peace Party of New York (Swarthmore College Library, Swarthmore, Pennsylvania). Cited hereafter as Woman's Peace Party Collection.

17. Press Release, February 13, 1916, Woman's Peace Party Collection.

18. J. Salwyn Schapiro to Crystal Eastman, undated, Woman's Peace Party Collection.

19. Crystal Eastman, "Speech Before the Balch-Angell Lecture Series," December 21, 1917, Woman's Peace Party Collection.

20. Crystal Eastman, "Shall We Change the Name?," Woman's Peace Party Collection.

21. Crystal Eastman to Mrs. Leigh French, February 28, 1917, in Correspondence File of the Woman's Peace Party Collection.

22. *New York Times*, October 31, 1917, p. 6.

23. Crystal Eastman to Louise Bryant, "Message to the All Russian Congress of Peasants' Soviets," February 26, 1918, Woman's Peace Party Collection.

24. Margaret Lane to George Plimpton, November 17, 1918, Woman's Peace Party Collection.

25. Elinor Byrnes to Katherine Devereaux Blake, April 23, 1919, Woman's Peace Party Collection.

26. Jane Addams to Margaret Lane, December 19, 1917, Woman's Peace Party Collection.

Notes

27. The correspondence between Jane Addams and Lillian Wald is in the Lillian Wald Collection, New York Public Library.

28. Lillian Wald to President Wilson, April 6, 1917, Wald Collection.

29. Crystal Eastman, "Proposed Statement to the Press," June 15, 1917, p. 2, in the American Union Against Militarism Collection (Swarthmore College Library, Swarthmore, Pennsylvania). Cited hereafter as American Union Collection.

30. Lillian Wald to Crystal Eastman, August 28, 1917, American Union Collection.

31. Lillian Wald to Jane Addams, August 14, 1917, Lillian Wald Collection, New York Public Library.

32. Minutes of the American Union Against Militarism, August 30, 1917, American Union Collection.

33. Ibid., November 26, 1917, American Union Collection.

34. Lillian Wald to Jane Addams, November 13, 1917, Wald Collection.

35. Minutes of the American Union Against Militarism, November 26, 1917, American Union Collection.

36. Crystal Eastman to Oswald Garrison Villard, November 16, 1917, American Union Collection.

37. Crystal Eastman to Jane Addams, November 28, 1917, correspondence file, Woman's Peace Party of New York (Swarthmore Peace Collection, Swarthmore, Pennsylvania).

38. Crystal Eastman to Oswald Garrison Villard, November 16, 1917, American Union Collection.

39. Lillian Wald to Felix Adler, June 4, 1918, Wald Collection.

40. Max Eastman discussed the trial in his second volume of memoirs; see Chapters XII, XIII, and XVIII in *Love and Revolution*. Also, Max Eastman, "The P.O. Censorship," *The Masses*, IX (September 1917), 24.

41. John Reed, "Free Speech," *The Masses*, IX (July 1917), 23.

42. Oswald Garrison Villard, *Fighting Years: Memoirs of a Liberal Editor* (New York: Harcourt, Brace, 1939), p. 328.

43. Crystal Eastman, "Proposed Announcement to the Press," September 24, 1917, American Union Collection.

44. Crystal Eastman to Henrietta Rodman, February 17, 1919; Crystal Eastman to Ida Rauh, February 21, 1919, Woman's Peace Party Collection.

45. Crystal Eastman, "Alice Paul's Convention," *The Liberator*, IV (April 1921), 10.

CHAPTER 6. THE NEW WOMAN?

1. Waterman, "A Critical Study of Susan Glaspell's Works . . . ," p. 257.

2. Susan Glaspell to Anne Bergel, October 23, 1936, in Walter Prichard Eaton Collection (University of Virginia Library, Charlottesville).

3. Neith Boyce to Mabel Dodge Luhan, June 16, ?, Hapgood Collection.

4. Ida Rauh, *And Our Little Life* . . . (New York: Bookman Associates, 1959).

5. *New York Times*, January 21, 1923, Part II, p. 6; January 25, 1923, p. 6; March 22, 1923, p. 19.

6. Crystal Eastman, "Alice Paul's Convention," p. 10.

7. Max Eastman, *The Liberator*, I (March 1918), 1.

8. Crystal Eastman, "News Report from Hungary," *The Liberator*, II (July 1919), 35.

9. Crystal Eastman, "In Communist Hungary," *The Liberator*, II (August 1919), 9.

10. Crystal Eastman, "The Socialist Party Convention," *The Liberator*, III (July 1920), 25, 29.

11. Max Eastman, *Love and Revolution*, p. 180, footnote. Eastman noted, in an interview with me in September 1966, that he did not realize how much or how well Crystal wrote. His re-reading of her unpublished writings on feminism, for example, gave him reason to doubt the judgment printed above.

12. Crystal Eastman, "Pandora's Box or What Is Your Trouble?" (unpublished manuscript, n.d.), in possession of Max Eastman.

13. Max Eastman, *Love and Revolution*, pp. 504–505; Freda

Notes

Kirchwey, *The Nation*, CXXVII (August 28, 1928), 123–124.

  14. Sinclair, *The Emancipation of the American Woman*, pp. 343–344.

  15. Dell, *Homecoming*, p. 242.

  16. Max Eastman, *Enjoyment of Living*, p. 291.

  17. Hapgood, *A Victorian in the Modern World*, p. 395.

  18. Dell, *Intellectual Vagabondage*, p. 139.

  19. Max Eastman, *Enjoyment of Living*, p. 392.

  20. Dell, *Intellectual Vagabondage*, p. 139.

  21. Crystal Eastman, "Modern Adventures in Maternity" (unpublished manuscript, n.d.), p. 1.

  22. Glaspell, *The Road to the Temple*, p. 239.

  23. Dell, *Intellectual Vagabordage*, p. 165.

  24. Crystal Eastman, "Modern Adventures in Maternity," p. 2.

  25. Glaspell, *The Road to the Temple*, p. 174.

  26. *Ibid.*, p. 183.

  27. *Ibid.*, p. 174.

A Note on Sources

THIS BOOK has drawn upon all of the published and unpublished writings of the Village feminists. All important citations appear in the footnotes. The amount of unpublished material is not as abundant as the historian would wish. Crystal Eastman's unpublished autobiography and essays were in the possession of her brother Max Eastman when I read them. Neith Boyce's unpublished writing is at Yale University, Neith Boyce and Hutchins Hapgood Papers, Collections of American Literature, Beinecke Rare Book and Manuscript Library. Henrietta Rodman has left no collection of her correspondence or unpublished writings. Ida Rauh is still living; although I saw her in 1966 and have written to her since, I have not seen any of her unpublished material. Some letters of Susan Glaspell have been preserved in the Clifton Waller Barrett Library, University of Virginia, but this is a very slight collection. Her biographer, Arthur E. Waterman, informs me that the autobiographical data on her are sparse and that her stepchildren have not provided much help in this area.

Floyd Dell's papers are at the Newberry Library, Chicago, and contain much useful information about all of the people of the Village community in the 1910's as well as many fragments of Dell's own writings. Max Eastman died in 1970, and Indiana University is presently collating his papers. Other important collections for this book were the Provincetown Players Papers in the Research Library of the Performing Arts, New York Public Library at Lincoln Center; the Lillian Wald

A Note on Sources

Papers at the New York Public Library, which contain the correspondence between Miss Wald and Jane Addams and provide many insights into the problems faced by the American Union Against Militarism during the war as well as the personal conflicts between Miss Wald, Miss Addams, and Crystal Eastman; and the Woman's Peace party, New York Branch Papers and the American Union Against Militarism Papers, both at the Swarthmore Peace Collection, Swarthmore College.

Two dissertations have been written on subjects of this study: George T. Tanselle's "Faun at the Barricades: The Life and Work of Floyd Dell" (Northwestern University, 1959) and Arthur E. Waterman's "A Critical Study of Susan Glaspell's Contributions to Modern American Drama" (University of Wisconsin, 1956); the latter study was published in 1966 as Volume 101 in the Twayne series on American writers. Both studies emphasize the literary, rather than the cultural, importance of the writers' views, but they offer the reader an overview of the literary output of both writers and the thematic nature of their work.

Autobiographies

Many of the Greenwich Village group published their autobiographies. The most helpful have been: George Cram Cook, *Greek Coins* (New York, 1925); Floyd Dell, *Homecoming* (New York, 1933); Max Eastman, *Enjoyment of Living* (New York, 1948) and *Love and Revolution* (New York, 1964); Joseph Freeman, *An American Testament* (New York, 1936); Susan Glaspell, *The Road to the Temple* (New York, 1927); Hutchins Hapgood, *A Victorian in the Modern World* (New York, 1939); Harry Kemp, *Tramping on Life* (New York, 1922); Mabel Dodge Luhan, *Movers and Shakers*, Volume 3 of *Intimate Memories of Mabel Dodge*

A Note on Sources

Luhan (New York, 1936); Ida M. Tarbell, *All in the Day's Work* (New York, 1939); Oswald Garrison Villard, *Fighting Years: Memoirs of a Liberal Editor* (New York, 1939); Mary Heaton Vorse, *A Footnote to Folly* (New York, 1935); and Art Young, *On My Way* (New York, 1928).

Feminist Writings

The primary writings of the feminists studied in this book are:

Neith Boyce, "Enemies" in *The Provincetown Plays* (New York, 1916).

George Cram Cook and Susan Glaspell, "Suppressed Desires" in *The Provincetown Plays* (New York, 1916).

Floyd Dell, *Intellectual Vagabondage: An Apology for the Intelligentsia* (New York, 1926); *Janet March* (New York, 1923); *King Arthur's Socks and Other Village Plays* (New York, 1922); *Love in Greenwich Village* (New York, 1926); *Love in the Machine Age: A Psychological Study of the Transition from Patriarchal Society* (New York, 1930); *Moon Calf* (New York, 1957); *The Outline of Marriage* (New York, n.d.); and *Women as World Builders: Studies in Modern Feminism* (Chicago, 1913).

Charlotte Perkins Gilman wrote extensively on the role of women in modern society. One especially useful article for this discussion was "The Waste of Private Housekeeping," *Annals of the American Academy of Political and Social Sciences* (November 1917), pp. 123–130. Mrs. Gilman's book *Women and Economics* (New York, 1898) is also fundamental.

The work of Susan Glaspell used here includes *A Jury of Her Peers* (London, 1927); *Fidelity* (Boston, 1915); *Plays* (Boston, 1920); *The Verge* (Boston, 1922); and *The Visioning* (New York, 1911).

A Note on Sources

Ida M. Tarbell's *The Business of Being a Woman* (New York, 1912) and *The Ways of Woman* (New York, 1915) offer a contrasting portrait of the role of women. Mary Heaton Vorse's play *I've Come to Stay* (New York, 1918) also provides examples of feminist heroines typical of the genre.

Magazines

Three major Village journals are rich in material: *Four Lights: An Adventure in Internationalism* (New York, 1917–1918); *The Liberator* (New York, 1918–1921); and *The Masses* (New York, 1911–1917). Specific articles in these and other magazines are cited in footnote references in the text.

Newspapers

The *New York Times* was especially helpful for its detailed coverage of Henrietta Rodman's activities. There were, for example, more than thirty references alone to the teacher-mother controversy during 1914–1915. The *Times*'s treatment of the Feminist Alliance was also good.

Secondary Sources

The most helpful secondary studies were Daniel Aaron, *Writers on the Left* (New York, 1961); Jessie Bernard, *Academic Women* (University Park, Pa., 1964); Sophonisba P. Breckinridge, *Women in the Twentieth Century: A Study of Their Political, Social and Economic Activities* (New York, 1952); Gertrude Bussey and Margaret Tims, *Women's International League for Peace and Freedom, 1915–1965* (London, 1965); Oscar Cargill, *Intellectual America* (New York, 1941); Edward Carpenter, *Love's Coming of Age* (New York, 1911); William E. Carson, *The Marriage Revolt* (New York, 1915); Eleanor Flexner, *Century of Struggle: The Woman's Rights Movement in the United States* (Cambridge, 1959); Inez

A Note on Sources

Haynes Irwin, *The Story of the Woman's Party* (New York, 1921); David Kennedy, *Birth Control in America: The Career of Margaret Sanger* (New Haven, 1970); Ellen Key, *The Morality of Woman* (Chicago, 1911); Aileen S. Kraditor, *The Ideas of the Woman's Suffrage Movement, 1890–1920* (New York, 1965); Christopher Lasch, *The New Radicalism in America, 1889–1963: The Intellectual as a Social Type* (New York, 1965); John William Leonard, ed., *Woman's Who's Who of America, 1914–1915* (New York, 1914); Robert Jay Lifton, ed., *The Woman in America* (Boston, 1965); Ferdinand Lundberg and Marynia F. Farnham, *Modern Woman: The Lost Sex* (New York, 1947); Henry F. May, *The End of American Innocence* (New York, 1959); William L. O'Neill, *Everyone Was Brave: The Rise and Fall of Feminism in America* (Chicago, 1969); Albert Parry, *Garrets and Pretenders: A History of Bohemianism in America* (New York, 1960); Margaret Sanger, *Woman and the New Race* (New York, 1920); Andrew Sinclair, *The Emancipation of the American Woman* (New York, 1965); and Coreea M. Walsh, *Feminism* (New York, 1917). The literature on feminism in the 1910's is still sparse. The current generation's interest in the subject has given rise to a spate of anthologies on women, but few, if any, have treated the Greenwich Village community.

Index

(171)

Index

23; feminist heroines in her fiction, 34–36, 38, 42–43; and Provincetown Players, 89, 91–92

Gold, Mike, 123

Goldman, Emma, 63–65, 135, 143

Greenwich House Settlement, 13

Greenwich Village, 3, 7–8, 120, 126, 133; as an intellectual community, 135–137

Hapgood, Hutchins, 19–22, 42, 87, 127–129, 132

Harry (Boyce), 119

Haywood, Bill, 4

Heidelberg, Max, 52

Henry Street Settlement House, 101

Hillquit, Morris, 4, 95, 106

Hollingworth, Dr. Leta, 82–83

Homecoming (Dell), 127

Howe, Julia Ward, 96

Intellectual Vagabondage: An Apology for the Intelligentsia (Dell), 127

Johnson, Hiram, 122

Kellogg, Paul, 101

Kun, Bela, 121–122

Lane, Margaret, 106

League of Women Voters, 116–117, 126, 145

Lewisohn, Ludwig, 92–93

Liberal Club, 3, 16, 85–86, 88

Liberator, 95, 111, 121–123

Lippmann, Walter, 136

Love in the Machine Age (Dell), 76

Luhan, Mabel Dodge. *See* Mabel Dodge.

Lusk Law, 120

Marx, Karl, 10, 135

Masses, 4, 8, 51, 53, 63–67, 69–76, 81–84, 95, 101, 112, 121

McKay, Claude, 13, 123

Men's League for Woman Suffrage, 73

Millett, Kate, 150

Minor, Robert, 123

(173)

A NOTE ON THE AUTHOR

June Sochen was born and grew up in Chicago, Illinois. After undergraduate work at the University of Illinois and the University of Chicago, she studied at Northwestern University and received a Ph.D. in history. Miss Sochen has also written *The Unbridgeable Gap* and edited *The Black Man and the American Dream* and *The New Feminism in Twentieth-Century America,* and is at work on a study of American women thinkers and activists in the twentieth century. She is now Professor of History at Northeastern Illinois University.